TAKE MY WORDS

OTHER BOOKS BY HOWARD RICHLER

The Dead Sea Scroll Palindromes
(Robert Davies Publishing, 1995)

TAKE MY WORDS

*A Wordaholic's Guide to
the English Language*

HOWARD RICHLER

RONSDALE PRESS
1996

TAKE MY WORDS
copyright © 1996 Howard Richler

RONSDALE PRESS
3350 West 21st Avenue
Vancouver, B.C., Canada
V6S 1G7

Set in New Baskerville: 11 pt on 14
Typesetting: Julie Cochrane
Printing: Hignell Printing, Winnipeg, Manitoba
Cover Design: Ewa Pluciennik

The paper used in this book is Miami Vellum. It is recycled stock containing no dioxins. It is totally chlorine-free (TCF) as well as acid-free (therefore of archival quality). The paper is made from at least 10% post-consumer waste.

The publisher wishes to thank the Canada Council and the British Columbia Cultural Services Branch for their financial assistance.

CANADIAN CATALOGUING IN PUBLICATION DATA
Richler, Howard, 1948–
    Take my words

    ISBN 0-921870-42-6

    1. English language—Etymology.   2. English language—humor.   3. Literary recreations.   I. Title.
PE1574.R52 1996   422   C96-910387-5

For my wife and editor-for-life, Ruth

CONTENTS

INTRODUCTION

"I N THE BEGINNING was the Word." So begins the Gospel according to Saint John. The moral genesis of our species can be traced to words, for they are what make us human. Words are the building blocks of language. Through words we derive ideas and through ideas we evolve. Through words we designate objects by giving them names. Through names we gain a subjective existence and a form.

Lytton Strachey wrote that "of all the creations of man language is the most astonishing." I concur with Mr. Strachey and in writing *Take My Words*, I hope to impart the miraculous nature of language.

Language is probably our greatest natural resource, but the average person knows very little about it. In fact, much of what people believe they know about language is merely folklore. Many think that meanings of words are immutable. Wrong. In Chapter 2, "Fair is Foul and Foul is Fair," and Chapter 10, "Never Say Die or Cadaver," I explain how the meanings of words are forever shifting.

Language is shrouded in many myths. For example, many words have folk etymologies that may be fanciful but not factual. Legend has it that the word "crap" derives from one Thomas Crapper, the inventor of the modern flush toilet. *The Oxford English Dictionary (OED),* however, has a reference to a "crapping ken," or water closet, in 1846, when the inventor-to-be was but a lad of nine. The subject of folk etymologies is covered in Chapter 4—"Language can be Derived very Deviously." Similarly, what is common knowledge about quotations is invariably wrong. This is covered in Chapter 16—"You Can't Trust Anybody over or under Thirty not to Misquote."

The operative thematic link in my book, I believe, is the word

"surprise." By being surprised one is learning and being enter-
tained concurrently. For example, we may assume that gestures
we employ are universal. In Chapters 20 & 21, I explain that they
are not. The inherently transitory nature of language is always a
source for much that is surprising about it.

English is fast becoming the *lingua franca* of the global village.
There are actually far more people who use English as a foreign
language than there are native speakers. In fact, there are now
more students of English in China than there are people in North
America. The *Oxford Companion to the English Language* lists over
400 varieties of our multi-varied mother tongue (one of them,
Quebec English, is discussed in Chapter 33). Yet most people
whose first language is English do not appreciate the special
resource they possess by virtue of having English as their mother
tongue. We are privileged to read the greatest writer of all time,
William Shakespeare, in his native language. Also, the *Oxford
English Dictionary,* arguably the greatest work of scholarship in the
history of humanity, is an English treasure. Due to the existence
of this dictionary, more is known about the history of the English
language than that of any other language in the world. The goal
of this book is to convey to the reader the richness and excite-
ment inherent in the English language and its potential to be
used recreationally.

The sheer size of the English vocabulary, its wealth of
homonyms, and its myriad borrowings create wonderful condi-
tions for wordplay. In "fun" topics, such as puns (Chapters 22 &
23), palindromes (Chapter 25), rhyming puzzles (Chapter 27),
malaprops (Chapter 18), spoonerisms (Chapter 19) and oxy-
morons (Chapter 17), readers will be asked to participate in the
literary process through wordplay exploration.

Wordplay should not be seen as mere whimsy. For those who
believe that wordplay is trivial, I suggest they reread Chaucer,
Shakespeare, Carroll and Joyce. Wordplay also has a didactic component. Canadian John S. Crosbie, founder of the International
Save the Pun Foundation, said, "Show people how to have fun
with words, and they may be motivated to read. It's one approach

to solving the problem of functional illiteracy." The stress in all forthcoming chapters will be on the entertainment value of language. To make the process interactive, many chapters include puzzles. Puzzling is perhaps the only genre of literature which calls on the active participation of the reader.

But beware before you participate in the language cabal. For as language maven William Safire warned, "if you get hooked on the study of the language, you are in that sorority, or fraternity, for life."

Most of the chapters are drawn from my "Speaking of Language" column found in the Books Section of Montreal's English daily, *The Gazette*. I would like to thank Books Editor Bryan Demchinsky for his gentle yet firm editorship, and for his friendship. I'd also like to thank the dynamic editorial duo, my wife Ruth and our friend Linda Schwartz, for their impeccable work and for turning the arduous editorial process into a fun activity.

PART I

WORDS, WORDS, WORDS

POLONIUS : What do you read, my lord?

HAMLET: Words, words, words.

Perhaps if Hamlet were not a Dane from the Middle Ages but rather an Anglophone living in the late twentieth century, there would have been no tragedy of *Hamlet*. He would have been too busy reading the approximately 616,500 words of the *Oxford English Dictionary*, by far the world's largest vocabulary list. Having somewhat of an antic disposition, he probably would have spent every waking moment perusing the 21,728 pages in twenty volumes of the said dictionary, which traces the usage of every word in the English language since the year 1000.

With his poetic bent, I'm sure the Prince of Denmark would have concurred with Oliver Wendell Holmes, Sr. who stated, "When I feel inclined to read poetry, I take down my dictionary. The poetry of words is quite as beautiful as the poetry of sentences."

1

ENGLISH IS NICE
AND FEISTY AND THAT'S NO
POPPYCOCK

W HEN PEOPLE OBJECT to a new meaning a word has
acquired, they invariably point to the history of the
word—its etymology—to support their position. The older meaning, however, is not necessarily the correct meaning. The word
"decimate" originally meant to "reduce by one-tenth," and it
derived from Latin, where it meant to "kill every tenth man as a
punishment for mutiny." Originally, "nice" meant "stupid" or
"promiscuous," and "silly" meant "blessed" or "happy." The modern meanings of many words bear little resemblance to their original sense. Indeed, many "nice" words have beginnings more in
keeping with the original lascivious connotation of "nice." To
demonstrate the ribald voyage of some words, I've orchestrated
the following vignette:

By all accounts the *seminar* was a *petard*. Asked to describe the
performance of Professor Harris, the kindest description of him
was "*feisty*." One *hysterical* critic *testified* that the Professor had "lost
his *fizzle*," another characterized Harris' thesis as "*poppycock*." The
luncheon served in the *Orchid* Salon was catastrophic. The *pumpernickel* was steely, the *partridge* rancid, the *avocado* was purple, the
aubergine green, and the *vanilla* ice cream had a peculiar after-
taste. Within 24 hours six of the unlucky diners were on *penicillin*.

From an etymological point of view, the described event has nothing to do with academia or food. The origins of all the underlined words reveal sullied connections with "unmentionable" body parts and their unseemly emanations:

SEMINAR—comes from the the Latin *seminarium,* or plant nursery. *Seminarium* is derived from the Latin *semen,* which means seed.

PETARD—as in Hamlet's "'oist with his own petard," was an explosive device which had a tendency to explode prematurely on its deviser. It derives from the French *peter* and the Latin *pedere,* both of which mean to break wind.

FEISTY—appeared as a noun, breaking of wind, and as a verb, to break wind, in the thirteenth century. A fisting dog was a contemptuous term for a cur.

HYSTERICAL—derives from the Greek *hysterikos,* which means "suffering in the womb." It was felt women were more prone to emotional disturbance because of malfunctions in their wombs.

TESTIFY—is borrowed from the Latin *testis,* testicles. In ancient times, a man would testify by placing his hand not on his heart, but on his cherished testicles. It was felt that if he lied, he would become impotent.

FIZZLE—The first definition of "fizzle" in *The Oxford English Dictionary (OED)* is "the action of breaking wind quietly." Like feisty, it derives from the word "fisten," to fart. There is a usage of fizzle in 1532 with the meaning "to fart noiselessly and unobtrusively," a Renaissance equivalent to the modern SBD (silent but deadly).

POPPYCOCK—comes from the Dutch *pappekak,* which means soft dung. The *kak* part comes from the Latin cacare, to defecate.

ORCHID—grew out of the Greek word for testicles, *orchis,* because of the supposed resemblance of its double root to two hairy testicles.

PUMPERNICKEL—This coarse bread is the progeny of the unholy marriage of two German words, *pumpern* (to break wind) and *nickel* (a goblin or devil). It was said that if you ate pumpernickel you'd fart like the devil.

PARTRIDGE—originates from the Greek word *perdesthai*, which means "to fart." The whirring partridge wings were said to make a sound akin to the breaking of wind.

AVOCADO—The ultimate avocado ancestor is *ahucatl*, testicle, from the Aztecan language, Nahuatl. The Aztecs felt that not only was the fruit shaped like a testicle, but that it had aphrodisiac properties. To the Spanish conquistadors, *ahucatl* sounded like *avocado*, the Spanish word for advocate.

AUBERGINE—has had an exotic etymological odyssey as an anti-fart vegetable. Sanskrit *vatinganah* refers to the lack of gas it produces. Sanskrit *vatinganah* became Persian *badingan*, then Arabic *al-badinjan*, then Portugese *beringela*, then Catalan *alberginia*, which became French *aubergine*, which has been adopted by English.

VANILLA—*Caveat emptor*, ye vanilla ice cream lovers, for vanilla, etymologically, is a little vagina. Vanilla is an extract from the Spanish *vainilla*, which means flower or pod. *Vainilla*, in turn, comes from the Spanish word *vaina*, which means sheath. *Vaina* derives from the Latin *vagina*, which means sheath for a sword. It was used lewdly as a term for the female reproductive passage.

PENICILLIN—is a derivative of the Latin word for tail or paintbrush, *penicillus*. This is an allusion to the bushy nature of its spores. In Latin, penis originally meant tail or brush, and only by extension did it come to represent the male sex organ. Etymologically speaking, a pencil is a little penis.

Alexander Pope wrote: "True wit is nature to advantage dressed,/what oft was thought but ne'er so well expressed." While it may be the mission of metaphor and euphemism to adorn words with new meanings, it is the calling of etymology to disrobe them.

2

FAIR IS FOUL AND
FOUL IS FAIR

O NE OF THE SOPHOMORIC jokes making the rounds in the early sixties explains the difference between a "good" girl and a "nice" girl as "the good girl goes to a party, goes home, then goes to bed, while the nice girl goes to bed first then goes home."

From an etymological perspective, this naughty sense of "nice" is correct. Chaucer's usage of nice in *Romance of the Rose* in the year 1366 suggests unchaste behaviour: "Nice she was, but she meant no harm or slight in her intent." In Shakespeare's *Love's Labour Lost,* the connotation is lascivious: "These are compliments, these are humours that betray nice wenches that would be betrayed." In *Antony & Cleopatra,* "nice" refers to amoral behaviour: "When my hours were nice and lucky men did ransom lives." The word "nice" evolved from the Latin word *nescius,* which meant "ignorant." It has enjoyed many meanings along its etymological odyssey. It has referred to all sorts of "unchristian" behaviour including promiscuity, extravagance and decadence. Early in its evolution it had an unmanly taint, being somewhat synonymous with timid, shy, fastidious, dainty and effeminate. Ironically, its modern meaning, being synonymous with pleasant, was the last one to develop. This connotation did not emerge until late in the eighteenth century. It was not until 1828 that Noah Webster saw fit to equate "nice" with "pleasant."

"Shrewd" is another word whose sense has ameliorated. It probably derives from the mouselike shrew, common in English forests, who will do combat for the tiniest morsel and will top off a meal by eating the vanquished foe. As one can see, this makes the taming of one no small feat. By the fifteenth century it had been used to mean "wicked," "dangerous," "ugly" and "grave." In the sixteenth century it came to mean "deceitfully cunning," and it is from this pejorative sense that the modern "astute" meaning emerged. The word "brave" has also taken an upward path. Originally it meant uncivilized or savage, having evolved from the Vulgar Latin *barbus,* which itself derives from the Latin *barbarus.*

While some words have "improved" with age, the opposite tendency (of taking on negative connotations over time) has been more common.

Originally, a "silly" person was blessed and happy due to an innocent nature. The word "silly" comes from the German *selig,* which means happy. The Middle English word "seely" meant good or happy. Although the meek may inherit the earth, they are not overly respected before they claim their inheritance. To be silly originally made one deserving of compassion and sympathy. This implied helplessness, and since important people are not seen as being helpless, silly came to mean insignificant and trivial.

"Daft" has undergone a similar regression. It started out meaning "mild" or "gentle," and only in the fifteenth century did it fall from grace and mean "stupid." A cousin of "daft," the word "deft" has managed to keep its meaning positive. Daft is a not uncommon surname in Leicestershire, and notwithstanding the shift in meaning, Dafts have not sought to change their names.

Originally, "notorious" had no pejorative connotation and simply meant "well-known." Its descent is probably due to the company it kept. It was used often to describe a liar, and by the seventeenth century it had itself acquired a negative connotation. A similar situation is happening, in reverse, with the noun "attitude," which has taken on a negative hue even without the accompanying adjective "bad." The stock of "lewd" and "villain" has also cascaded. "Lewd" once referred to being a member of the laity, as opposed to the clergy. Since the masses were uncultured, lewd came to take on this meaning, and since the uncultured were "vulgar," it took on this sense as well. "Vulgar" itself meant "belonging to the common people" and only took on a lascivious meaning in the eighteenth century.

The evolution of "villain" also shows a contempt for the masses. Originally, it referred to a low-born rustic. In feudal England, a "villein" (its original spelling) was a serf who was a virtual slave to his lord and was regarded more as a commodity than a person. The similarity between vile and villain may have contributed to its demise. Charles Lamb inaugurated the use of villain as a play's antagonist in 1822.

Probably the most cynical metamorphosis is that of the word "cretin." Originally, it meant "Christian" and was used charitably to describe a mentally deficient person. One's imperfection enabled one to receive more of God's grace. But it was the fate of the "clowns of God" to be reduced to mere clowns.

Are no meanings fixed, you ask? Is not "good" good and "bad" bad? Not according to the *OED*. One of the definitions of "bad" is "possesssing an abundance of favourable qualities, of a musical performance or player: Going to the limits of free improvisation, of a lover. . . ."

Macbeth's witches were right. Foul is, indeed, fair.

3

THERE'S A LOT OF
FOOD FOR THOUGHT AT
A FOOD SYMPOSIUM

F RENCH GASTRONOME Anthelme Brillat-Savarin wrote, *"Dis-moi ce que tu manges, je te dirai ce que tu es"* which has been transformed into the modern maxim, "you are what you eat." Someone who is down-to-earth is dubbed as "meat and potatoes;" an energetic person is said to be "full of beans," possibly because of the potential for flatulence. Food has always been a metaphor for our likes and dislikes. We designate outstanding things or people as the "cream of the crop," or as the "best thing since sliced bread." Something special is called "icing on the cake." A loved one is referred to as the "apple of one's eye" or as a "honey." The word "honeymoon" derives from the Germanic custom during the Middle Ages, when a married couple would drink honey wine during the first month of marriage.

Often an adjective is used to give a negative sense to a food term, as in "sour grapes," "hot potato," "small potatoes," or "bad apple." Terms like "lemon" and "crab" denote negative qualities in themselves. Although in the case of the word "crab," etymologists are divided between considering it a reference to the sour crab apple, or to the seemingly anti-social behaviour of shellfish crabs, secreted away in the crevices of rocks.

Molière said, *"il faut manger pour vivre et non pas vivre pour manger;*" eat to live, don't live to eat. A 1994 conference in Montreal entitled "Health and Pleasure at the Table" questioned Molière's existential dictum. At this international symposium, academics and food professionals debated the ever-changing nature of consumer tastes and the myriad challenges facing the food industry. A "narrative meal," with a Greek motif, was served. According to symposium organizers, it encompassed more than the "sharing of good food and wine," as its "vision of life [was one] that Socrates, Hippocrates, and Epicurus would have easily shared." Epicurus believed that pleasure consisted in right living, which leads to a healthy body and mind. This idea of pleasure was perverted by others to refer to a life of luxury. Out of this connotation came the word "epicurean," which originally referred to a gluttonous appetite but has come to refer to refined and tasteful enjoyment. The Romans admired the Greeks' love of wine so much that they adopted the Greek god of wine, Dionysus. They referred to him by his alternative name, Bakkhos, which they spelled as Bacchus. Each year, the Romans honoured Bacchus in a wild orgy of eating and drinking called a Bacchanalia. From this ritual comes the word "bacchanal," which refers to a drunken reveler.

The origin of some expressions relating to food is surprising. Eating "humble pie" originally was humbling because it referred to the "umbles," the entrails of a deer that servants in medieval England were reduced to eating, while their masters dined on the more succulent parts. The term "cold shoulder" is another expression with a medieval origin. While an important visitor might be regaled at a castle with a piping hot meal, a commoner would be served a cold shoulder of mutton.

The period between 1500 to 1700 was a time of ubiquitous geographical exploration for England. The English language gladly accepted as refugees a great variety of foods and beverages. Here are some of the language additions that filtered in: Arabic, alcohol and coffee; Basque, anchovy; Chinese, tea; Dutch, spinach; Greek, pumpkin; Italian, macaroni and ravioli; Malay, ketchup; Portuguese, molasses; Taino (Haitian), potato; Wolof (West African), banana. During this period, the Aztec language, Nahuatl, provided us with some of our mainstay food names. "Tomato" came to us via Nahuatl as "tomatl," and was brought back to Spain by the marauding Conquistadors. In North America, it was not until the early part of the nineteenth century that tomatoes were grown as a food plant. Previously, they were grown mainly for decoration, because it was widely believed they were poisonous, and by some puritanical souls that they bred licentiousness.

The English dictionary has become a literal melting pot of exotic foods from around the globe. The twentieth century has seen a great explosion of new foods into the English language. Some examples are Mexican, taco and burrito; Yiddish, knish and kishke; Greek, moussaka and souvlaki; Japanese, sukiyaki and teri-yaki; Italian, saltim bocca and canneloni; Chinese, won ton; and Middle Eastern, falafel. Sometimes the exact source of a food is not known. For example, rumaki, an appetizer consisting of chicken liver, found its way into dictionaries in the early '60's but its origin is listed only as Oriental.

And the food "additives" keep mushrooming. The *Random House Word Menu,* under the heading "prepared dishes," lists foods such as tzaziki, baba ghanouj, chimichanga, and fajitas, which have become part of the dining landscape, yet are not fixtures in English language dictionaries.

There is one glaring non-entry from the *Word Menu* at which I take umbrage as a Quebecer. Poutine was omitted.

Fill in the blanks with the appropriate fruit or vegetable.

1. Cool as a _____
2. Red as a _____
3. _____ of his eye
4. _____ ear
5. Baseball argument _____
6. The _____ of Wrath
7. Spill the _____
8. _____y keen
9. like two _____ in a pod
10. _____ Republic

4

LANGUAGE CAN BE DERIVED
VERY DEVIOUSLY

A) WHAT TYPE OF animal is a titmouse? B) What colour is a greyhound? If your answers were mouse and grey respectively, you're wrong for A and not necessarily right for B, as a greyhound comes in colours other than grey. A titmouse is a bird and its second syllable derives from the German meise, a small bird. The "grey" in greyhound in Old Norse meant coward, and is a reference to its ability to flee from danger.

The names of both of these animals are examples of folk etymologies. In etymology, as in other fields, people feel uncomfortable with the unexplained. The explanations that are put forward, while imaginative, often bear little resemblance to the truth.

Throughout the ages, etymology suffered much ridicule. Voltaire described it as "a science where the vowels mean nothing, and the consonants very little at all." Nineteenth-century linguist Samuel Pegge wrote that "nothing in the world is more subject to the power of accident, of fancy, of caprice, of custom, and even absurdity, than etymology." The Reverend A.S. Palmer wrote in *Folk-Etymologies* in 1890 that etymology was prone to "unskillful necromancers" who "spirit the wrong soul in the wrong body." Etymology is subject to much guesswork. The *Oxford Companion to the English Language* states that "as with information in the fossil record of paleontology, what is known of the origin and development of a word . . . is a matter of chance."

Etymology is also subject to the prejudices and cultural assumptions that the etymologist brings to the study. For example, the word "girl" originally was gender neutral and referred to a child of either sex. A mid-fifteenth century text refers to "knave-gerlys," "male children." Based on the premise that females are more garrulous than males, some etymologists claimed that girl derives from the Latin *garrula,* the word for talkative. No less a great thinker than the lexicologist Noah Webster saw "girl's" derivation from the Latin *gerula,* "a young woman employed in tending children."

Some of the popular misconceptions of word origins are the subject matter of *Devious Derivations* (Crown, 1994) by Hugh Rawson. Aside from the entertainment value of unmasking false beliefs, Rawson believes folk etymologies are worth studying because the meaning ascribed to many words has been based on mistaken beliefs about their origins. Often a foreign word is recast in a form that seems more familiar. The Spanish *cucuracha* was transformed into cockroach even though the insect has no roots to poultry or to the roach, a type of freshwater fish. Sometimes, as with the word hangnail, the original meaning of a word is betrayed. Etymologically, a hangnail does not hang. Originally, the word was "angnail" and the "ang" referred to the pain it caused—as in "ang/uish."

Imaginary eponyms figure colourfully in the history of folk etymology. Rawson relates that notwithstanding a prolonged historical search, the annals of history do not reveal a Dr. Condom of prophylactic infamy. The origin of condom is unknown. The word shyster, according to legend, derives from a shady nineteenth-century New York lawyer named Scheuster. His existence, like that of his professional counterpart Dr. Condom, is illusory. Rawson tells us that the "word is basically German, deriving from *scheisser,* an incompetent fellow, particularly one who cannot control his bodily functions." The root word *scheisse* is scatological in nature.

It is common knowledge that the word "cop" is an acronym for Constable on Patrol or Constabulary of Police. It many be common knowledge but it is also wrong. Etymologically, a cop is one who "cops" or catches thieves. One folk etymology I've heard often is that the derogatory term for an Italian, "wop," derives from the acronym "without papers" or "without passport" and was a reference to the way new arrivals came to America. The actual source of the word is the Neapolitan *guappo,* a term for a somewhat disreputable dude.

Folk etymologies tend to be shrouded in grand tales. One such story surrounds the word "sincere," which legend tells us derives from the Latin *sine cera,* "without wax." William Sherk, in *500 Years of New Words,* tells us that in ancient Rome "workmen in marble quarries would rub wax into the cracks in marble columns to make them look whole." Sherk and others have claimed that a marble merchant's sign, *sine cera,* was a way of stating that his product was "without deception." Rawson, for one, doesn't buy this legend. Unless an archaeologist one day uncovers an actual *sine cera* sign he's going with a much simpler theory. He believes that sincere derives from the Latin *sincerus,* meaning pure and untainted.

5

MOVE OVER MICHAEL, MATTHEW'S THE #1 KID IN TOWN

M A, IT AIN'T FAIR. Whereas brother Edward's name means "guardian of wealth," as Howard, I get to watch over mere hogs (Hogward) or ewe (Eward). I shouldn't complain. You could have named me Claude, "lame" in Latin; Calvin, "bald" in Latin; or Ulysses, "hater" in Greek.

Actually, uncomely meanings are more likely to be found in surnames than forenames. Examples of such are: Kennedy, "ugly head;" Boyd, "sickly;" or Campbell, "crooked mouth." Worse off still is the O'Sullivan clan, whose name denotes not an ugly feature, but the lack thereof. Gaelic reveals a kinship between the O'Sullivans and the one-eyed Cyclops.

After the Norman Conquest, the most common male names in England were Henry, John, Richard, Robert and William. These five names, which represented 38% of male names in the twelfth century, climbed to 64% of usage by the fourteenth century. The most used name through this period was William. For females, the names Mary, Elizabeth, and Anne made up about half of the names in England in the seventeenth and eighteenth centuries. The oldest parish records in the United States show that between 1648 and 1699 the three most popular male names, in order, were John, William, and Thomas. For females the leader was Elizabeth, followed by Mary and Anne.

The use of saints' names only started to be in vogue in the tenth century. This is why, of the five most common male names during the Middle Ages, biblically derived John is the only non-Germanic representative. John takes many forms in other languages. Some are easily recognizable, like Jean, Juan, Johannes, Sean, Ivan and the Serbian Jovan. Others, like the Irish Sean, Gaelic Iain, Welsh Evan and the Finnish Juhana, are not as obvious. Some derivatives of John also require translation: whereas John in German is Johannes, Johnny becomes Hans or Hansel.

Surnames were first used on a regular basis by the Romans. A Roman's first name was of least importance. Julius Caesar's first name was not Julius but Gaius. Julius was in fact his clan name. Concomitant with the fall of the Roman Empire was the collapse of surnames. The practice seems to have been revived in France in the eleventh century and later in other parts of Europe. A limited number of "Christian" names were being doled out at the baptismal font. Something had to be done to distinguish between the endless Johns and Marys. Enter surnames. In England, two events led to the imposition of surnames. In 1379, the Crown levied the dreaded poll tax, which meant that the name of everyone sixteen or over had to be registered. The Statute of Additions in 1413 dictated that a person's name, occupation, and domicile had to appear on any legal document. John, who was known as John Robertson because of his father Robert, and as John Smith because of his occupation, and as John Armstrong because of his strength, and as John Atwater because he lived near the river, had to choose one of the four nomenclatures as his fixed surname.

Notwithstanding that motherhood is a matter of fact and fatherhood a matter of opinion, it is the supposed father's name and not the actual mother's name that has been honoured in a male-dominated world. Names that end in "son" or "sen," like Johnson and Jansen, or begin with "O," "Mc," "Mac" or "Fitz," like Fitzpatrick, are examples of patronyms. The prefix "Fitz" is actually an Anglo-Norman corruption of French "fils" and was used to denote bastardry. In days of yore 'twas better to be a bastard son of a Somebody than a legitimate son of a Nobody.

Many children today bear hyphenated names, carrying their heritage from both parents. It will be interesting to see how nomenclature will be handled when our hyphenated children meet and marry others similarly hyphenated. When Mary Papadopolous-Schwarzkopf and John Monnypenny-Rodriguez bear a child, will Billy have to endure the appelation Billy Papadopolous-Schwarzkopf-Monnypenny-Rodriguez? Poor Billy. The exam will be over and he'll still be writing his name.

I never asked my parents why my brother Edward and I were both given "ward" names. Perhaps it's because we were both born in hospital wards. Actually, I'm sure they selected our names because they liked them. In any case, *Montreal Gazette*-reading parents cast their ballots in the Dec. 31, 1994 "Babies of the Year" feature and here are the results:

It would appear that long time favourites like William, John and Mary are no longer in vogue. Of the 1058 babies highlighted (533 boys and 525 girls), only two were named William, although there was one Billy. There were three Johns, but Mary, Elizabeth and Anne were all shut out. For boys, the leading names were Matthew (24), Michael (15), Nicholas and Jonathan (14) and Daniel (13). For girls, the most popular name was Sarah (21), followed by Jessica (19), Stephanie (16) and Amanda (12).

Though the names have changed, some things still remain the same. Not surprisingly, there was much more diversity in girls' names than in boys' names. This has been the pattern for hundreds of years.

Match the following names with their meanings.

1. Amanda	(a)	beautiful
2. Amy	(b)	bee
3. Ann	(c)	beloved
4. Barbara	(d)	crown
5. Daniel	(e)	fame-bright

6.	Edward	(f)	farmer
7.	George	(g)	foreign
8.	Henry	(h)	fortunate guardian
9.	Joel	(i)	God is God
10.	John	(j)	God is gracious
11.	Linda	(k)	God is judge
12.	Melissa	(l)	grace
13.	Michael	(m)	home rule
14.	Robert	(n)	lily
15.	Stephen	(o)	who is like God?
16.	Susan	(p)	worthy to be loved

6

IT'S HARD KEEPING
UP WITH THE SMITHS IN
ANY LANGUAGE

"WHAT'S IN A NAME?" Juliet ponders in *Romeo and Juliet*. With respect to surnames, she discovers to her chagrin, that the answer is "plenty." Though she and Romeo can be as one, the Capulets and the Montagues cannot co-exist. But it was not only the surnames of noble families that had significance. Surnames emerged to differentiate between individuals, and each one told a story. The surname Jackson meant you were the son of Jack; the surname Wright meant you knew how to write.

In days of yore it was common for a son to earn his living in the same manner as his forefathers and so it was logical for a surname to reflect the family metier. Some obvious names of this genre are Smith, Hunter, Taylor, Baker and Cook. The meaning of some surnames like Fletcher (a maker of bows and arrows), Barker (a tanner), and Fuller (clothes cleaner) has been lost through the ages.

Smith is the most common surname in North America and England and has a sizeable lead over its nearest rivals, Jones and Johnson. It is also popular in its many foreign forms: Ferrier and Lefebvre (French), Ferraro (Italian), Herrero (Spanish), Haddad (Syrian), Kovacs (Hungarian), Schmidt (German), Kowalski (Polish) and Kuznetsov (Russian).

Why there are so many "Smiths" in the world is a bit of a mystery, for it wasn't so common an occupation as to warrant so many members. After all, there were probably more shepherds than smiths in olden days, yet Smith is by far the more common surname. The plethora of Smiths is probably due to the enhanced status the profession assumed during wartime.

Curiously, in the Middle Ages a person could be given a surname based on his neighbour's profession. Since literacy was not the norm, many tradesmen had pictograms outside their businesses. A striped barber pole is a legacy of this tradition. In *The Mother Tongue*, Bill Bryson relates that the symbol denoting a wine merchant was a bush, and hence his hapless neighbour George might be dubbed George Bush.

Some surnames derive from location. If someone lived near a lake, well, ash tree, or hailed from London, his surname might be Lake, Atwell, Ashley or London. He was more likely to have a surname denoting a smaller population centre like Middleton rather than London. Being John London living in London would not help distinguish you from all the other Johns hailing from London, whereas coming from Middleton and being named such could. If John from London moved to Middleton then he might be dubbed John London.

Considering the supposedly celibate nature of people bearing surnames like Monk, Bishop, and Levesque (*évêque* means bishop in French), these names have been passed on to succeeding generations in large numbers. This is because part of the original name may have been shed with the passage of time. For example, Bishop at one time may have been "bishop's man." A surname like Pope, however, suggests a nickname as the source.

Aside from patronymics, occupations and places, nicknames are the other major source of surnames. The Romans, who introduced surnames, can also take credit for instituting nicknames. Orator Marcus Tullius Cicero's family name was not Cicero, but Tullius. Cicero is a nickname meaning "wart on the nose," and was an appellation probably inherited from a relative with an ugly proboscis.

Approximately 15% of Italian surnames are derived from nicknames. This practice is particularly prevalent in the rural south, where unpleasant attributes are captured in surnames. Machiavelli means "bad nails," Boccacio "bad mouth" and Scarsello "little miser." Noted film director Frederico Fellini's family name means "wicked" and journalist Oriana Fallaci's surname does not endow her with professional credibility—it means "fallacious." Most physical characteristics denoted in surnames are merely descriptive. Rossi, one of the most common Italian surnames, denotes redheadedness, as do the French surnames Leroux and Rousseau. The colour white gets much mileage throughout the world in names like Bianchi (Italian), Weiss (German), Byelov (Russian), Gwynne (Welsh) and Leblanc and Blanchard (French).

Europeans have been loathe to tamper with surnames. In England, name changes have been restricted to names like Shittle and Piddle. France actually dictates which names can be changed. If your surname is Fromage (cheese) a switch is permitted, but if you're a Chevre (goat) it is not allowed. By contrast, changing one's surname in North America is quite common. Some immigrants use the opportunity of being in a new land to doff surnames with unpleasant meanings. One can hardly blame a Greek immigrant with the surname Koloktronis (bullet in the ass) for exercising this option.

A spate of celebrities like John Wayne (originally Marion Morrison) and Tony Curtis (originally Bernard Schwartz) changed their names to sound more macho, or more "American." Sometimes only the pronunciation is changed. Ronald Reagan had the pronunciation of his surname changed from "Reegan" to "Raygun." This elicited LBJ's quip that his "beagles might turn into bagels."

In many societies, to have one's name referenced from one's mother was an insult of the "yo mama" variety. Matronyms, names derived from a mother, are not very common and are found with any frequency only among Ashkenazic Jewry. Some examples are Dvorkin, derived from Deborah; Sorkin, derived from Sarah; and Rifkin, derived from Rivke (Rebeccah).

The use of surnames among the Jews of Europe did not become common until the beginning of the eighteenth century. Previously, most Jews were known by their name as well as their father's name, as in Isaac ben ("son of") Abraham. European governments wanted their Jewish subjects to have permanent surnames to facilitate taxation and conscription. Many Jews thus adopted surnames that have pleasant connotations such as Goldberg, "gold mountain" and Rosenthal, "rose valley." In some domains, one had to pay officials to get a positive-sounding name. Refusing to pay left some with unpleasant names such as Galgenstick, "gallow's rope," and Eselkopf, "donkey's head."

Québecois surnames are marked by a lack of diversity. The large numbers of Tremblays, Gagnons, Roys, etc. are due to an original immigration to New France of under 10,000, and a paltry rate of immigration after the British conquest. By far the most common Québecois surname is Tremblay. The clan patriarch, Pierre Tremblay, came to New France in the mid-seventeenth century. He lived in Beaupré and begat four sons, three of whom migrated north to Baie St. Paul. Pierre's sons proved to be more fruitful than their father and collectively sired 49 children. Before long the entire North shore—especially the area around Baie St. Paul—was teeming with Tremblays. Today, in the Saguenay area, Tremblays account for almost 10% of the populace.

Another prolific Québecois family is the Gagnons. Three Gagnon brothers came to New France in 1635 and settled around Chateau-Richer. They weren't quite as fecund as the Tremblay lads and averaged only eleven children each. Mathurin Gagnon got a late start when he married at the age of forty. His bride Francoise Boudeau was thirteen years old and she went on to produce fifteen children. When his fifteenth child was born, Mathurin was seventy-one years old.

Curiously, certain Québecois families are linked genealogically. Two sets of pairs are Roy-Desjardins and Hudon-Beaulieu. At one time the surnames were *Roy dit Desjardins* and *Hudon dit Beaulieu*. It is supposed that the secondary names were originally added as nicknames to help differentiate individuals.

As a defenceman for Les Canadiens, Eric Desjardins may have had an added reason to protect goalie Patrick Roy: he was probably kin.

Match the celebrities with their original identities.

1. Israel Baline
2. Charles Bunchinsky
3. James Baumgarner
4. Issur Danielovitch
5. Arnold Dorsey
6. Reginald Dwight
7. Frances Gumm
8. Herbert Khaury
9. Benjamin Kubelsky
10. Michael Phillip
11. Roy Scherer
12. Bernard Schwartz
13. Richard Starkey
14. Robert Zimmerman

(a) Jack Benny
(b) Irving Berlin
(c) Charles Bronson
(d) Tony Curtis
(e) Kirk Douglas
(f) Bob Dylan
(g) Judy Garland
(h) James Garner
(i) Rock Hudson
(j) Engelbert Humperdinck
(k) Mick Jagger
(l) Elton John
(m) Ringo Starr
(n) Tiny Tim

7

STICKS & STONES
MAY BREAK YOUR BONES BUT
CURSES CAN KILL YOU

I N THE BEGINNING was the Word, and the Word was a Curse. In the third chapter of Genesis the serpent, Eve, and Adam all suffer God's ire. The serpent is the first victim. He is told that he is "cursed above all cattle" and will suck sand for the rest of his days. Eve's sentence is, "I will greatly multiply thy pain and thy conception: in pain thou shalt bring forth children." Adam's yoke is also heavy: "Cursed is the ground for thy sake; in toil shalt thou eat of it all the days of thy life."

The Bible does have benedictions as well as maledictions, but God's munificence aside, the blessings are boring. Here are some examples extracted from Leviticus 26: "I will give you peace in the land . . . and make you fruitful . . . and establish my covenant with you." Compare this ho-hum blessing to the following ill wishes: "I will send pestilence among you and you shall be delivered into enemy hands. . . . You shall eat the flesh of your sons and daughters. . . . I will make your cities waste and bring your sanctuaries unto desolation. . . ." No contest.

Ashley Montagu, in *The Anatomy of Swearing*, sees swearing as the "generic" form of speech, and cursing as a type of swearing. He believes that the development of swearing preceded that of cursing. "Expletives [and] maledictions . . . preceded the speech-making and later rituals involved in the deliberate apportioning of the fate of an enemy." Montagu states that one swears when one seeks immediate relief; thus swearing is conjugated in the present tense. Since cursing entails the desire of ill eventually to befall the target of the curse, its language is couched in the future tense.

The ancient Greeks and Romans did not swear much because of the power held in curses. Montagu says that "when one has available so effective a resource as . . . cursing, it is . . . unnecessary to go to the trouble of belabouring one's enemy with mere words." Cursing has been the prerogative of the clergy and a rather dangerous practice for the laity. Exodus 21:17 states "And he that curseth his father, or his mother, shall surely be put to death."

Islam imposes the same sentence on anyone who curses the prophet Mohammed. The *fatwa,* the religious decree of execution, was issued against author Salman Rushdie by Ayatullah Khoumeini for allegedly cursing the Prophet in *The Satanic Verses.*

The curse ritual can be as important as the actual words of the curse. In some parts of Ireland, the following rite is still practised. Twelve or thirteen round stones are placed in a basin while the execrator intones a curse. Care must be taken, for the penalty of letting a stone slip is having the curse boomerang on its deliverer. According to Irish folklore a curse *must* land somewhere. The statute on cursing limitations is quite long. A curse can float in the air for up to seven years before striking its intended victim. Italy also boasts a stone curse. In the Italian version, the curser maliciously jettisons a stone into a river while anathematizing the following: "I cast not away this stone, but cast away the well-being and good fortune of (Signor X) so that his well-being should flow away with the coursing water so that he may no longer enjoy any good!"

In many societies there is a relationship between a curse and the evil eye. If one sees a baby and gushes, "What a pretty girl," it's advisable to follow the admiration with some verbal abuse, lest the wrath of envious demons be unleashed. In modern day Hungary some people still let loose, in triplicate, some prophylactic spittle upon praising a child.

In *The Lost Art of Profanity* written in 1948, author Burges Johnson relates how Samoans use cursing as a means of crime detection. A Samoan who discovers fruit has been stolen from his garden goes to an assemblage and bellows, "May fire blast the eyes of the man who stole my bananas!" The identity of the thief is revealed by his trembling at the prospect of the prophecy's fulfillment.

Cursing practices around the world vary greatly. To effect a curse, the aborigines of Australia don't talk, they point. A stick or bone is pointed at a victim if one is present, or at his house if he is absent. H. Basedow, in *The Australian Aborigine*, states that the victim, "overcome with . . . terror, begins to fret . . . and death will inevitably be the outcome. . . ." Pregnant Maori women in New Zealand have to contend not only with the danger to their unborn children of smoking; swearing and cursing are also deemed to be deleterious to their babies' health.

Nowadays, colourful cursing or swearing is rare, which is not surprising considering the inventory of cusswords is threadbare; there are barely a dirty dozen. This is not a new refrain. H.L. Mencken commented that among returning GI's from WW II the "repertory of invective was tragically thin and banal." In 1948, Burges Johnson bemoaned that "vituperation—the communication of feeling by word symbols hot from the furnace—should no longer be an art or even a common skill."

8

FIFTY YIDDISH WAYS
TO CURSE YOUR NEIGHBOUR

S IGMUND FREUD believed that verbal wit serves as a safe outlet
for repressed impulses. This is true: if one's aggression is
likely to cause retaliation, it is wise that your slings and arrows be
linguistic rather than physical. Cursing has proved to be a useful
outlet for oppressed minorities. This is borne out by the colourful
curses to be found among chronically subjugated groups such as
gypsies, Afro-Americans, the Irish and Eastern European Jews.

The Jews who lived in Eastern Europe before WW II had no
problems cursing creatively. They had the advantage of speaking
Yiddish, which according to Joe Singer in *How To Curse In Yiddish*,
was "a tongue seemingly fashioned exclusively for the quip, rag,
and riposte." Yiddish curses should not be confused with the
Hebraic curses of the Bible. Hebrew curses were deadly serious,
whereas there is a humorous thrust to almost all of the Yiddish
variety.

Maurice Samuel in *In Praise of Yiddish* states: "The Jewish people, being physically defenseless, had two recourses short of sui-
cide; it could contain itself in silent patience . . . or it could vent its
rage upon the world in impotent intramural rages until it recov-
ered its balance. . . . It had only faith and its wits to fall back on,
the faith was deep, the wits—and the wit—were lively."

One usually associates cursing with malevolence, but Yiddish cursing can be downright jocular. This is because the Yiddish curser usually does not believe in the power of his or her execrations. Yiddish cursing developed into a choreographed activity where satisfaction was gained by ejaculating an imaginative curse. Many of the curses were improvised and were designed to exhibit the verbal celerity of the execrator. Singer says that Yiddish curses "first lull you with their innocence, then flatten you with the punchline." An example of this verbal feinting is "May you lose all your teeth except one—so you can have a toothache!"

While traditional Yiddish curses were generally humorous, this is not to say that ill will was never directed towards others. Life was hard and interactions did not take place in laid-back bucolic settings with fiddlers on roofs. An acerbic wit and a good delivery could earn one much respect. But in cursing your neighbour or your competitor at the market, you could dream that the object of your scorn was the Tsar or some other oppressor.

Yiddish cursing was, by and large, the domain of women. The men enjoyed sanctuary in holy studies but this escape was not afforded to Jewish women. When a husband devoted most of his time to religious study, the wife became the family provider. The only profession open to her was work at the market. To release anxiety in this hectic workplace, she learned to "curse like a market-woman."

One would never merely say "drop dead" in Yiddish. The simplest way of expressing this wish was "Into the earth with you!" Since a child could only be named after a deceased, you could kill with kindness by saying "May they name a baby after you!" One's death wish could be couched in blessings, as in "May God bless you with a son so smart he learns the mourner's prayer before his Bar Mitzvah speech!" and "May you be spared the indignities of old age!" Wishing disease or pain on someone was a popular theme, especially if the individual was wealthy. Benedictions took sudden u-turns and mutated into maledictions: "May he own ten shiploads of gold—and may all of it be spent on sickness." One peculiar ill wish was "A cholera in your bones!" It must have been felt that bone cholera was more uncomfortable than the run-of-the-mill variety. Other ill wishes included: "May you become famous—they should name a disease after you," "May your blood grow so healthy, your leeches' leeches need leeches" and "May you be such a fast healer, new boils keep growing over your boils!"

You wouldn't know it listening to Henny Youngman jokes, but mothers-in-law were not the bane of men, but of women. As mentioned earlier, a man had the means of escape, but the wife could be constantly besieged by her mother-in-law in the home or at the market. Two examples of this genre are, "May your mother-in-law treat you like her own daughter and move in with you" and "May your husband's father marry three times so that you have not one but three mothers-in-law!" Anorexia nervosa was not a common ailment in the Jewish community of yore. A plump figure was a sign of affluence and a selling point for the local matchmaker. "May you never develop stomach trouble from too rich a diet" was definitely not a blessing but it sounds desirable next to "May you grow four stomachs like a cow, so that you get four times the belly-ache and four times the heartburn."

I have thus far eschewed vulgar curses but I'd like to end with a ditty, scatological in nature: "May you fall into the outhouse just as a regiment of Cossacks finishes a prune stew and twelve barrels of beer!"

9

THE GREATEST
WORDMAKER

I F YOU HAD ASKED an early sixteenth-century English writer
why English literature had not produced any masterpieces for
over a century, you probably would have been told that it was
because his mother tongue was second-rate. English possessed an
impoverished vocabulary and was not considered to be a proper
medium for the expression of scientific, abstract, or philosophical
ideas. Sir Thomas More wrote *Utopia* in Latin in 1516, but it was
not translated into English until 1551. By then it had already been
translated into German, Italian and French. In the last quarter of
the century, however, attitudes began changing. Writing in
English was seen by an increasingly literate society as a sign of
patriotism. In 1582, English scholar Richard Mulcaster said that
Latin reminded him of England's "thralldom and bondage," and
that "I love Rome, but London better, I favor Italie, but England
more, I honor the Latin, but I worship the English." Also, the
vocabulary of English was swelling. One of Mulcaster's students,
poet Edmund Spenser, bequeathed us neologisms such as
"blatant," "braggadocio," "violin," and "shiny." There were many
prolific word progenitors in this era, but one name stands out.
Etymologist Ernest Weekly describes this wordmaker's contribution to phraseology as "being ten times greater than that of any

writer to any language in the history of the world." And this man's name was, of course, William Shakespeare.

Shakespeare used approximately 20,000 separate words in his works, which accounted for approximately forty percent of the then-available English vocabulary. He is credited in the *Oxford English Dictionary* with the first usage of over 1700 words, an amount that represents more than eight percent of the vocabulary he employed. George Gordon, in *Shakespeare's English,* commends the Elizabethans for their willingness to use "every form of verbal wealth." Shakespeare was fortunate to live at a time when the English language was very fluid. Gordon says Shakespeare was able to do what he liked with English grammar because it had no fixed rules and he "drew beauty and power from its imperfections."

Many words were created by the addition of prefixes and suffixes. "Premeditated" was first used in *A Midsummer Night's Dream.* "Useful" and "useless" were first used in *King John* and *The Rape of Lucrece* respectively. The word "amazement," which first appeared in *Titus Andronicus,* is one of the first uses of the suffix "ment" to form a noun from a Teutonic verb. As a language with deep Germanic roots English had a long tradition of creating new words through compounding, as German still does. Some of Shakespeare's contributions here are words like "barefaced," "hotblooded," and "lackluster."

If English lacked a word that could enhance his writing, Shakespeare invented the word, invariably one with a Latin root. In *Shakespeare's Language,* N.F. Blake points out that "Latinate words being polysyllabic are often rhythmic and mellifluous and Shakespeare used them and created them for this purpose." Shakespeare created the word "frugal" from the Latin *frugalis*— sparing or meagre, and its first use is in *The Merry Wives of Windsor*—"I was then frugall of my mirth." The word "castigate" derives from the Latin castigare—to correct—and makes its debut in *Titus Andronicus.* "If thou didst put this soure cold habit on to castigate thy pride, 'twere well." "Obscene" derives from the Latin *obscenus,* whose first meaning was "adverse," or ill-omened.

Shakespeare first employs it in *Richard II:* "In a Christian climate soules refin'de should shew so heynous, black, obscene a deed." The word "radiance" comes from the Latin radiantia—brightness. It is first seen in *All's Well That Ends Well:* "In his bright radience and colaterall light, must I be comforted."

But of course Shakespeare's contribution to the English language transcends his creation of individual words. The story is told of a student who, after seeing *Hamlet* for the first time, opined that the play was nothing more than a collection of cliches. However, when Shakespeare coined expressions like "brevity is the soul of wit" and "the primrose path," they were unpolished gems.

Shakespeare's contribution to English phraseology is ubiquitous. British writer Bernard Levin has pointed out that we are all unwitting Shakespeare citers—"without rhyme or reason." If you are "in a pickle" because you've been "eaten out of house and home" and even your "salad days" have "vanished into thin air," you are quoting Shakespeare. You've been "hoodwinked" and "more sinned against than sinning." No wonder you're not "playing fast and loose" and haven't "slept a wink" and are probably "breathing your last." It's "cold comfort" that you're quoting Shakespeare. If you "point your finger" at me, "bid me good riddance" when you "send me packing," and call me a "strange bedfellow," a "laughing-stock," "the devil incarnate," a "sorry sight," "eyesore," and a "stone-hearted," "bloody-minded" "blinking idiot" and wish I were "dead as a door-nail" after you put a "plague on both [my] houses," I would say you possess neither a "heart of gold" nor "the milk of human kindness," especially considering I'm your own "flesh and blood." It's a "foregone conclusion" you are quoting Shakespeare.

Match the Shakespearean expression to the play from which it comes.

1. All the world's a stage	(a) Hamlet
2. Bated breath	(b) Henry IV
3. The better part of valour is discretion	(c) The Tempest
4. Brave new world	(d) Romeo & Juliet
5. Breathe life into a stone	(e) King Lear
6. Brevity is the soul of wit	(f) King John
7. Budge an inch	(g) Julius Caesar
8. The dogs of war	(h) All's Well that Ends Well
9. Fair play	(i) As You Like It
10. Foregone conclusion	(j) The Merchant of Venice
11. Full circle	(k) The Taming of the Shrew
12. A plague on both your houses	(l) Othello

PART II

VICES & DEVICES OF LANGUAGE

Sometimes language is employed not to communicate, but to deceive, cajole, confuse, or exaggerate in an attempt to gain an edge in the game of life. The uses of language are not always benign. Language may be the greatest tool humanity owns, but a tool can be used just as easily to destroy as to build. George Orwell argued that "the great weapon of power, exploitation, manipulation, and oppression is language."

In this section, I'll discuss some of the uses and abuses of language.

10

NEVER SAY DIE
OR CADAVER

"**F**OR THOSE PROCEEDING to the cemetery, please follow the coach," intoned the speaker funereally. There was something jarring about the use of the word "coach" to refer to a conveyance for a cadaver. It didn't square with my association of the word with Cinderella's transport to the ball. Later, I was surprised to discover that the word "coach" has been used for over half a century as a euphemism to help deal with the unpleasantness of the last obscenity—Death. "Coach" is but one of the many euphemisms employed in the funeral industry. When the euphemisms acquire the precise meanings of the words they have replaced, they, in turn, are replaced by untarnished terms.

The term "mortician" started to replace undertaker in the 1890's. A 1920's waggish definition said a mortician was the person who buried his euphemistic counterpart in selling land for the living—a realtor. "Undertaker" itself had originally been a euphemism, and came from the term "general contractor," one who undertook contracts. The fact that this contractor was literally "taking one under" the earth probably had something to do with the word undertaker gaining such wide usage. Around 1925, the American funeral industry undertook a public relations campaign via newspapers and phone directories to have "mortician" replaced by the more user-friendly "funeral director."

"Cemetery" was introduced to replace the harsher-sounding "graveyard." It derives from the Greek *koimeterion,* which means dormitory. Cemetery, however, may be on the way out. Increasingly, one hears the term "memorial park" employed for the final resting place.

Coffins were supplanted by caskets by the 1860's. American writer Nathaniel Hawthorne was not a supporter of casket's usage. He wrote, "Caskets!—a vile modern phrase which compels a person of sense and good taste to shrink more disgustfully than ever from the idea of being buried at all." Good taste maven Emily Post, however, accepted casket (albeit with grave reservations): "In spite of the fact that the word coffin is preferred by all people of fastidious taste, and that the word casket is never under any circumstances used in the spoken language of these same people, it seems best to follow present-day commercial usage and admit the word casket to these pages."

The ancient gods were the first euphemistic subjects. Temperamental sorts, they were capricious and easily provoked to anger. Hence, great care was taken to avoid their wrath. To speak a god's name was possibly to invoke the awesome power of the deity. Therefore, circuitous references to these gods were devised. The Greek term *Hades* originally just referred to the ruler of the Underworld, and not the locale. It meant "the unseen one," and the not-visible deity's domain was only referred to as "down there." Because the Greek goddesses were nasty, they were referred to as *Eumenides,* the kindly ones, in the hope that this sycophancy would placate them.

Kind Words authors Judith S. Neaman & Carole G. Silver state that "we think of euphemisms for death as mere manifestations of our unwillingness to deal with it, but anthropologically these names are vestiges of our struggle against an adversary—a battle in which the weapons [are] words." We may think of the euphemistic "if anything should happen to me" as demonstrating our society's inability to countenance death, but interestingly, both ancient Latin and Greek have exact counterparts to it. In some cultures it is taboo to mention the name of the deceased, lest this act as a catalyst to summon the provoked spirit from the nether-world. If the departed must be referenced, he or she is mentioned in a roundabout manner by a term like "that one," as is employed by some Australian tribes. The Nandi tribe of East Africa have a euphemistic nomenclature at which I would take umbrage if I chanced to be the departed spirit. They reference the deceased as "rubbish."

The intent of many of the words to describe death is to make death less deathly, e.g. to "depart," to "pass on," to be "called home," and the definitive designation, to "pass away." "Pass away" has had an unusually long euphemistic currency, first being used in the Middle Ages. It works just as well for non-believers in an afterlife as it does for those who believe that a passing away is a passing on. It implies, like the term "fading away," a peaceful evanescent journey. Many of the slangish expressions for death, such as "push up daisies" and "croak," would appear to be callous and offensive. They are, however, a way of being cruel to be kind. The thrust, I believe, is to take the sting out of death. They are a way of saying "life must go on, so don't let death depress you unduly." Probably best known of these slang death references is the expression "kick the bucket." The "bucket" refers to a wooden frame from which the back legs of a recently slaughtered pig were suspended. A muscular twitch after death caused the pig to "kick the bucket." Notwithstanding this gruesome origin, the intent of this idiom is to take the solemnity away from death.

Euphemisms have the annoying tendency of not calling a spade a spade, but a subterranean cultivation intermedium. When employed by obfuscating governments, their true mean-ings must be unmasked. But when used as an attempt to soften the blow of a death and provide comfort to a mourner, their eva-sive nature is to be commended.

11

MONTREALER CRIES
"FOUL!" OVER PEA-FOWL

A DISPLAY CASE AT the Canadian Museum of Nature in Ottawa features a bird with resplendent plumage. The description explains that the MALE PEA-FOWL is spreading out his feathers to woo a PEA-HEN. I was informed of this avian cleansing in a letter from a reader of my *Gazette* language column who believes that calling a peacock anything but a peacock "is an example of excessive clean-up of the English language."

The original English name of the peacock was pea. In the fourteenth century it was formed into the compounds peacock (cock meaning male bird) and peahen (hen meaning female bird). The non-sex specific peafowl was a nineteenth-century construct. The non-use of the word "peacock" by the Canadian Museum of Nature is a Victorian Era vestige, when prudery deemed that the first line of defense against immorality was the regulation of speech. The Museum's avoidance of the word peacock is not only anachronistic, it is inconsistent, because its replacement, "peafowl," is gender-neutral, whereas "peahen" takes the feminine form.

When used pejoratively, the word "Victorian" conjures up an image of British prudishness. North American society, however, has been far more Victorian than the British in describing parts of the body. British Captian Frederick Marryat, in *A Diary In America* (1839), relates that when he came to the United States he was rebuked for asking a lady who had tripped whether she had hurt her leg. After regaining her composure, the injured party informed him that the word "leg" was never mentioned in front of a lady, and must be replaced with the word "limb." Henry Longfellow, in *Kavanagh* (1849), quotes from the prospectus of a fashionable American boarding school that "young ladies are not allowed to cross their benders in school." Some demented puritanical souls went as far as to cover the legs of pianos lest male passions be unleashed.

Can you think of a group of animals less alluring than poultry? Yet in North American society, several poultry parts became unmentionable. H.L. Mencken relates in *The American Language* (1919) that British writer W. F. Goodmane, while at an American dinner in the 1840's, was "not a little confused on being requested by a lady . . . to furnish her with the first and second joints of a chicken." Not all the coded chicken words are of such an old vintage. At our family dinners in the 1950's and 1960's, the choices consisted of white meat (breast) and dark meat (thigh) of a chicken.

Notwithstanding our "unmentionable's" origin being onomatopoeic (as in cockadoodledoo), by the year 1825 the term to describe a male bird had acquired an indelicate anatomical connotation in North America. This led to some peculiar "cockectomies." In the series of essays, *Sam Slick* (1838), by Canadian Thomas Chandler Haliburton, a young man informs a girl that her brother has become a "rooster-swain" in the Navy. Puerile humour about his family name drove the father of American novelist Louisa May Alcott to change it from Alcox to Alcott. For many ministers, the "cock crewing" of the Gospels became the unpoetic "rooster crewing."

Another animal referenced in the Bible that has fallen from grace is the ass. Nowadays, the word "arse" is used as a euphemism for the word "ass." This is ironic, because originally ass was used as a euphemism for the word arse. By the end of the eighteenth century, "ass" had become so sullied that the word donkey entered the English language.

In *Kind Words* (1983), authors Judith Neaman and Carole Silver explain that one of the main ways of euphemizing is "borrowing words from other languages—terms that are less freighted with negative associations." This has entailed eschewing short words of Anglo-Saxon stock in favour of polysyllabic imports. Writer Robert Graves, in *Lars Porsena* (1927), relates the story of a soldier wounded in the posterior who is asked by a woman visiting the wards, where he is injured. He replies, "I'm sorry, ma'am, I can't say. I never studied Latin."

Although the English language abounds in taboo words, Peter Farb in *Word Play* points out that their use is universal. Among the most prudish people on earth, according to Farb, are the Nupe of West Africa. "Indelicate subject matter must be expressed . . . by a word borrowed from another language. . . ." The Nupe tongue lacks any native procreative word and uses an Arabic derivative that means "to connect." Farb tells us that English has forced the elimination of innocent words from the vocabulary of native populations in North America. The Creek Indians of Oklahoma avoid their words *fakki* (earth) and *apissi* (fat) because they sound like two English taboo words. The taboo can work in reverse. The word "such" so closely resembles a four letter word in the language of the Nootka of Vancouver Island that teachers find it very difficult to convince their students to utter the English word in class.

A peacock is a peacock is a peacock. The eschewing of the word peacock by the Canadian Museum of Nature has cast a shroud of impropriety over an innocuous word. By doing so it provides an excuse for infantile humour.

Government and the military have brought obfuscating euphemisms to a new height (or depth). Match euphemisms to meanings.

1. aerodynamic personnel decelerator
2. collateral damage
3. core disruptive accident
4. exfiltration
5. freedom fighter
6. incontinent ordinance
7. incursion
8. interdiction
9. interrogation
10. negative economic growth
11. non-goal-oriented members of society
12. preemptive counterattack

(a) retreat
(b) bums
(c) blockade
(d) parachute
(e) torture
(f) unintentional killing of civilians
(g) guerilla
(h) meltdown
(i) first strike at enemy
(j) bombs that hit civilian targets
(k) recession
(l) invasion

12

KEEP IT SIMPLE, STUPID

H OW MANY WORDS does it take a civil servant to say "Do the important things first?" Answer: twenty-three, "The rate at which the objective is achieved should reflect the degree to which the organization has priorized that component of the plan."

The above language inflation comes courtesy of the Department of Fisheries & Oceans. The federal government commissioned the Ottawa firm *Prosebusters* to translate it into English. Mind you, *Prosebusters* is not your garden variety translator. It specializes in converting the language of bureaucrats, sometimes known as "bafflegab" or "gobbledegook," into comprehensible English sentences like "Do the important things first."

I know some of our more urbane readers are thinking to themselves, "What can you expect from the rubes in the Department of Fisheries?" Well, it doesn't get better in more "highbrow" domains. The following gem was mined from the Justice Department: "Active involvement has taken place concerning the departmental restructuring of the exercise through the formation of a branch committee to deal with and advise on all human resource aspects of the exercise." *Prosebusters* turned the above into the manageable "We have started a committee to help employees affected by transfers and layoffs."

Co-owner of *Prosebusters,* Cecilia Blanchfield, describes the language malaise as "toxic prose syndrome. People who used to be able to write clearly and eloquently become infected by other bureaucrats and they can't write anymore. It's like some cancerous growth develops on their brain and they just start producing bafflegab." She defines bafflegab as "the science of using words to protect your butt." *Prosebuster's* mandate is "to stem the growing tide of white-collar word crime." Though "appalled as a taxpayer," because most of their work involves rewording government literature, Blanchfield is "pleased as a business person." "People in government are scared, so they try to sugarcoat everything. They want to hide the truth as much as possible." Blanchfield says proper writing can often eliminate governmental language waste by over 60%. "They expand everything as much as possible. They blow it up, full of hot air, and we have to shrink it down to something real." For example, one ministry's convoluted sentence— "To make these determinations requires a flow of information that allows appropriate and timely action to be taken even in relation to activities that are consummated within a very short time span"—was reduced by 47% when *Prosebusters* changed it to "Good judgements require a steady stream of accurate information even when events happen quickly."

It appears our federal government has joined the comprehension bandwagon. The Department of Multiculturalism and Citizenship has spent $100,000 to produce a 55-page booklet entitled *Plain Language Clear and Simple.* The booklet advises those in government to write in a clear manner that is likely to be understood by its intended audience. It advises making only one point per sentence, each averaging fifteen words and no more than twenty-five words. Paragraphs should be limited to one idea and should not exceed five sentences. Clear and familiar words like "do," "help," and "try" should be favoured over "accomplish," "facilitate" and "endeavour." Unnecessary phrases like "notwithstanding the fact that" and "in the event of" can be replaced by "although" and "if" respectively.

What prompted this epiphany for clarity was a Statistics

Canada survey on literacy in Canada, which found that one in three Canadians has problems with everyday reading tasks. Shockingly, one in six Canadians "cannot determine how much medicine to give a child by looking at a bottle." It is not only governments whose communication skills need honing. All too often, the jargon used in particular fields leaves the uninitiated baffled. *Prosebusters* edited a book on battered women "which stated that women's ability to testify in some way is proportional to their own victimization process." *Prosebusters* changed this to the easily understood "the more frightened you are, the harder it is to speak out." The reading skills of the intended audience must be factored into the writing process. Parents would be better served if the report card said "Johnny could do better," rather than "academic achievement is not commensurate with individual ability."

In her book *In Defence of Plain English*, Canadian writer Victoria Branden decries the rampant "talking classy" syndrome, where people use polysyllables without any regard to their meaning. The use of plain words is seen as a sign of "inferiority and naivete." Unfortunately, this disdain for clarity even extends into the highest realms of academia. Patricia Nelson Limerick, a history professor at the University of Colorado, believes that miscomprehension has become an art form in academic circles. In a recent *New York Times* piece she said that if one doesn't understand an academic writer, the implicit message is "Too bad. The problem is that you are an unsophisticated and untrained reader. If you were smarter, you would understand me."

As an example of indecipherable prose, she quotes from Allan Bloom's *The Closing of the American Mind*. "If openness means to 'go with the flow' it is necessarily an accomodation to the present. That present is so closed to doubt about so many things impeding the progress of its principles that unqualified openness to it would mean forgetting the despised alternatives to it, knowledge of which makes us aware of what is doubtful in it." Professor Limerick asks, "Is there a reader so full of blind courage as to claim to know what this sentence means?" Ironically, Bloom's book was a jeremiad lamenting the mediocrity of the modern student. Now I understand what Jane Austen meant when her character Catherine Morland says in *Northanger Abbey,* "I can not speak well enough to be unintelligible."

Some academics see incomprehensible prose as a form of armour. How can a critic challenge the writer's position if he doesn't have the foggiest notion as to what the words mean? Limerick claims that the prophylactic use of obscure prose serves no purpose, for there is no danger, since tenure innoculates professors from the slings and arrows non-academics must constantly dodge. Limerick says that while it is accepted that today's college students have problems writing, "few seem willing to admit that the professors are not doing much better." She says it is difficult to persuade students to write clearly when they find little clarity in their assigned reading. In her closing paragraph, Limerick calls on fellow professors to jettison a writing style that conceals flaws "behind a smokescreen of sophistication and professionalism."

We should all follow the maxim of the first century A.D. rhetorician Quintillian who said, "One should not aim at being possible to understand but at being impossible to misunderstand."

Read the following bloated versions of some pithy proverbs and restore the proverb's concise nature.

1. If you retire with canines, you're prone to commence the next day alongside wingless blood-sucking insects of the order Siphonaptera.

2. Exist and let your fellow homo sapiens continue to be.

3. Consolidation effects erection of our personhood, whereas bifurcation effects our declension.

4. One-sixteenth of a pound of prophylactic is equivalent to sixteen ounces of alleviation.

5. While sugary condiments provide supereminence, it must be admitted that fermented grain provides greater celerity.

6. Never under any circumstances scrutinize the mastication orifice of a gratuitous herbivorous quadruped.

7. Pulchritude does not extend beyond the profundity of the epidermis.

8. Show extreme caution to those of Hellenic persuasion who are transporting goods for disposal on a non-charge basis.

9. Habitual or customary performance of what you advise in your homilies is advisable.

10. Penniless solicitors should not be expressing existential imperatives.

11. Just because one can engage in accelerated locomotion does not imply that one will be successful in concealing one's precise location.

12. He who administers to the somatic ailments of mankind should be applying balm to his own personhood.

13

BE P.C & KNOW
COSELF

HUMPTY DUMPTY: When I use a word it means just what I choose it to mean. Neither more nor less.

ALICE: The question is whether you can make words mean so many different things.

HUMPTY DUMPTY: The question is which is to be the master. That's all.

(*Through The Looking Glass* by Lewis Carroll)

LEWIS CARROLL realized that language not only reflects social change, it also shapes the change. For example, calling a woman a girl and a Black man a boy may be a tool to deny them adult status.

The term "politically correct" began as an expression to denote a non-offensive, multiculturally-oriented choice of language. Nowadays, its connotation is pejorative and it is usually implied in a sarcastic manner to reference a supposed enforced orthodoxy to which the so-called politically-correct individual would hold us. A few examples: feminist Andrea Dworkin characterizes "normal" men as violent and evil; legal scholar Catherine

Mackinnnon says freedom of expression must be suspended in order to end the subjugation of women. Leonard Jeffries, chairman of the Afro-American Studies Department at CCNY, says the world can be divided between "sun people" (Africans, Asians and Latins), and "ice people" (the rest of humanity). The former group is warm and humanistic, whereas the latter group is cold and materialistic. Several years ago, a Canadian Federal agency in its annual report advised Federal employees to eschew the use of the word "niggardly, a word of Scandinavian lineage meaning stingy, lest Blacks be offended."

The Official Politically Correct Dictionary & Handbook (Villard Books, 1992) by Henry Beard and Christopher Cerf, is a collection of some of the most outrageous neologisms and ideas advocated by the "culturally appropriate." One of the proposed amendments is spelling the word "dictionary" *dicktionary*, because Noah Webster and his ilk were patriarchal *DWEMs* (Dead White European Males) whose thoughts were dominated by the first four letters of the revised spelling. To radical proponents of Politically Correct (PC) terminology, a white, male, heterosexual power elite controls thought by controlling language. Western culture is seen as thoroughly racist, sexist and responsible for most of the world's evil. Disagreeing with this analysis demonstrates *false consciousness,* even if you're a member of the oppressed.

Other changes proposed include *efemcipate* for emancipate, *femhole* for manhole, *femstruate* for menstruate, and *wimmin* for women, although some prefer the word *womban*. Gone are dirty old white men. Get used to *sexually focussed, chronologically gifted, melanin impoverished individuals of the male persuasion.*

Beard and Cerf caution us that the term "politically correct" has been usurped by the racist, sexist, ageist, ableist, speciesist, sizeist power elite as a "tool for attacking multiculturalism," and therefore the term "politically correct" is no longer politically correct. This is disconcerting, for I found solace in discovering that I'm not balding and myopic, but *hair disadvantaged* and *optically challenged*. And who wouldn't prefer to be *vertically, horizontally and cerebrally challenged,* and *cosmetically different* over being short, fat, stupid and ugly?

On the other hand, sharing a *processed animal carcass* (steak) with your *domestic incarceration survivor* (wife) doesn't sound too appetizing. And don't think you're automatically PC if you're a vegetarian. Eating fruits and vegetables is kosher only if they became "separated from their parent plant either through the action of gravity or some other natural event. . . ." *Coself* is a gender-neutral substitute for "herself" or "himself," which was coined by feminist writer Mary Orovan, as in "Wilma advised Charlie to go f—k coself." *Enclosure* is the gender-fair substitute for sex, since it isn't phallocentric, like "penetration" and "insertion." Example: "Enclose yourself and the horse you oppressed by riding in on!" Beard and Cerf caution us that since postmodernist theory has "proved" that language is "the major force in constructing . . . reality," all social ills must take a backseat to correcting linguistic inequalities. Why does this sound "distinctly" familiar?

An unfortunate aspect of the pejoration of the term "political correctness" is that the emendatory use of language gets lumped with the egregious. "Birthmother" is an improvement over "real mother," as "flight attendant" is preferable over "stewardess." We should not forget that most language changes have been positive. In the sixties it was not unusual to hear health professionals referring to "idiots" and "imbeciles."

Name the non-politically-correct word that the following PC words and phrases are superseding.

1. achieve a deficiency	(a) emancipated
2. animal companion	(b) fail
3. cerebrally challenged	(c) girl
4. chronologically gifted	(d) meat
5. client of the correctional system	(e) old
6. domestic incarceration victim	(f) pet
7. efemcipated	(g) pregnant
8. melanin impoverished	(h) prisoner
9. ovarimony	(i) stupid
10. parasitically oppressed	(j) testimony
11. prewoman	(k) white
12. scorched animal carcass	(l) wife

14

NOBODY HAS
A MONOPOLY ON LINGUISTIC
INTOLERANCE

"MAN HAS BEEN defined," wrote Bergan Evans, "as a tool-using animal, but his most important tool, the one that distinguishes him from all other animals, is his speech." It is language that defines our humanity, our ability to create values. Through language we acquire that most valuable of possessions, a distinct identity. Tools can be used to build, but they can also be used to destroy. While language defines who we are, it also defines who we are not. Along with a sense of inclusion comes the need to exclude others. Intolerance to others has been manifested through language, through the antipathy to any language other than one's mother tongue.

It seems part of human nature to divide the world between the comprehensible Forces of Light—"Us"—and the unintelligible Forces of Darkness—"Them." The Greeks called foreigners "barbarians," because they thought their speech sounded like a stammering "bar-bar." Similarly, Genghis Khan's Mongol hordes were referred to by the Chinese as "Tatars," because they characterized their language as gibberish with a "ta-ta" sound. The Aztecs called their language "Nahuatl," which means pleasant-sounding, whereas other languages were characterized as stammering.

Anthropologists keep chancing upon societies whose names for themselves translate roughly as "the people," but whose designation for others is not so benign. Nor is this process restricted to preliterate peoples. The Germanic term *Deutsch* derives from the term *tiutisk*, which means "pertaining to the people." The Japanese word for foreigner means "stinking of foreign hair."

Ethnic adjectives are rarely complimentary. To take "French leave" is to go AWOL, to leave improperly. A "Mexican car wash" refers to leaving one's car out in the rain, and "Dutch courage" is alcohol-induced. Nor is this process restricted to English. One who mistreats the French language speaks *comme une vache espagnole,* and a pointless argument is *une querelle d'allemand.* In Germany, *nach Spanien verreisen,* going to Spain, means having an abortion, and *französische Krankheit,* French sickness, describes syphillis.

A nationality by itself, whether employed as a noun or a verb, can be an insult. In the Czech Republic, a Hungarian is referred to as a "pimple," Germans call cockroaches "Frenchmen," and the French call lice "Spaniards." The supposed niggardly nature of others is highlighted in such verbs as "jew," "gyp"(from gypsies) and "welsh."

When French gastronome Brillat-Savarin said, "You are what you eat," I don't think he meant to imply that French people were "frogs," or that German people were "(sauer)krauts." The French use the term *un rosbif* as a pejorative description of an Englishman. Ironically, the term *rosbif,* sometimes decried as a dreaded Anglicism, was originally a French word adopted into English after the Norman invasion. That most American of designations, "Yankee," comes from the Dutch *Jan Kaas,* meaning "John Cheese." Originally, it was an ethnic insult flung at New York colonists of Dutch heritage. It was used as a term of derision for the Dutch love of cheese.

People tend to feel that their particular language is superior. The French like to think of their language as the most beautiful and the most rational. Italians point to the musicality of their mother tongue, Germans stress the clarity of expression their speech provides, and Arabic speakers highlight the logicality and grammatic symmetry found in the classical form of their language. Languages are, however, inherently equal. There is nothing limiting about any language. All languages meet the myriad needs of their speakers. There are obviously structural differences among languages, but this is a question of what the particular language chooses as its foci.

It was believed in the nineteenth century that explorers would eventually discover a society with a primitive language, lacking in vocabulary and grammar, and highly dependent on gestures. Notwithstanding the "uncivilized" nature of a given society, no primitive language lacking complexity has ever been discovered.

French writer Harzic wrote that *"les Français ont une conviction innée dans la superiorité de leur langue"* (the French have an innate conviction of the superiority of their language). Linguistic chauvinism is equally rife among many English writers. Robert Clairborne, in *Our Marvellous Native Tongue,* goes so far as to say English is the "greatest" language, but he doesn't regard this statement as chauvinistic in nature.

The predominance of a language in a particular era proves nothing. By this rule, we would have to hold the absurd positions that seventeenth-century French is superior to present day French, and that American English is "better" than British English. Perhaps one day some objective criteria will be formulated that will allow us to evaluate the linguistic merits of different tongues. Until then, we are best holding to the tenet that all languages are equal. Anthony Burgess, in *A Mouthful of Air,* commented that "the emotions aroused by group loyalty obstruct the making of a judgement about language. When we think we are making such a judgement, we are often merely making a statement about our prejudices."

PART III

SAY IT AGAIN, SAM!

In the child's game Broken Telephone, a word or phrase is whispered quickly from one child to the next, with the result that what comes out of the last pair of lips is rather different from what went into the first pair of ears. Like life itself, language has a way of mutating, even when one speaks the same language as one's neighbour. Classical song lyrics, such as the Beatles' "The girl with kaleidoscope eyes" and Dylan's "The answer, my friends, is blowing in the wind," have been transmogrified respectively into "the girl with colitis goes by" and "the ants are my friends."

Communicating a point can fail for a variety of reasons. Some words carry different meanings for different individuals, making true communication all but impossible. Or a person may intend to say something and may believe that he has, when in fact he has said something quite different. Even when we gesture, the meanings of the movements can be misunderstood.

Communication is problematic enough when conversing with someone who shares your mother tongue. But when one doesn't possess a strong grasp of a non-native language, the results can be most interesting, sometimes hilarious, and occasionally horrific.

15

WHEN TRANSLATION FAILS,
IT MAY BOMB

"P*énétrez dans la voiture, restez en érection dans le siège et passez le ceinture au travers des cuisses.*" If you guessed "sex manual" as the source of the above, you are only partially correct. Before being poorly translated into French, it was the rather tame phrase from a car manual: "enter the car, sit erect in the seat and pull the belt across your lap."

What is lost in translating menus from English to French often is the desire for the meal. A finger sandwich loses its appeal when it is transformed into *"sandwich de doigts,"* as do sweetbreads and cocktail mixers when they are mutated respectively into *"pain doux"* and *"diluants."* A restaurant with a pirate theme had its "Virgin's Chicken Breast Sandwich" transmogrified into French. What emerged was an affront to chastity: *"sandwich de la vièrge à la poitrine de poulet."* These examples of pseudo-autoerotica and curious French cuisine were related to me by Paula Shannon of *Berlitz Translation Services.*

Corporate slogans, at times, have taken a beating when translated. *Pepsi's* famed slogan, "Come alive with the Pepsi generation," when translated by a Chinese newspaper in Taiwan emerged as the uninviting "Pepsi helps bring your ancestors back from the grave." When Ford first sold Model-T's in Russia, it recommended in a brochure to wash the car with "Ivory Soap." When translated into Russian the instructions advised using soap made from elephant tusks. In Scandinavian languages, the word for vacuum cleaner derives from its function of sucking up dust. Swedish-based Electrolux decided that its North American slogan should convey the powerful swooshing quality of its product. Thus emerged a slogan with rhyme but no reason: "Nothing Sucks like Electrolux."

Poor translations have created some peculiar political utterances. John F. Kennedy, during his well-remembered trip to Germany, wanted to express that the Berlin Wall was not only an affront to Berliners, but to freedom-loving people everywhere. In German, words for nationalities are not preceded by articles and Kennedy wanted to say *"Ich bin Berliner!"*—"I am a Berliner!" What Kennedy actually proclaimed was *"Ich bin ein Berliner!"* which translates as the somewhat less powerful "I am a jelly doughnut!"

Russian leader Nikita Khruschev was told during a television interview in the United States that he was "barking up the wrong tree," i.e., that he was wrong. Russians were outraged when this idiomatic expression was interpreted as their leader "baying like a hound." Former USA President Jimmy Carter, on a tour of Poland, wanted to say "I have a strong desire to know the Polish people." Through the ineptness of a translator, that "knowledge" came out stronger and more biblically than Carter intended. The message that emerged was "I desire the Polish people carnally."

Words that look the same in two languages often do not mean the same thing. English and French share many of these *faux amis,* "false friends," as they are called. There is *"sympathique/*sympathetic," where the French word means "agreeable" and not "sympathetic," and *"prétendre/*pretend," where the French verb means "to claim."

Linguist Mario Pei, in *The Story of Language,* relates how two of these French-English *faux amis* created some diplomatic stirs. The USA State Department took affront at a note from the French government that began: *"Nous demandons,"* because it was translated literally as a demand rather than a request. Once at the UN, a passage that described the collapse of Western Europe as "brutal" created much international tension until it was realized that it had been translated literally from French, where the idiomatic usage of *brutal* corresponds more to the English "serious" than to "brutal." A 1905 draft of a treaty between Russia and Japan was written in English and French. The English "control" and the French *contrôler* were treated as equivalent, notwithstanding the fact that in English the word connotes dominance, while in French it simply means "to inspect." The treaty nearly dissolved over a misinterpretation.

These misinterpretations seem trivial compared to one that may have contributed to the death of over 130,000 people. At the Potsdam Declaration on July 26, 1945, Japan was ordered to surrender unconditionally. In response, the Japanese Cabinet stated that Japan was giving the peace offer *mokusatsu,* which can mean "we are considering it," or "we are ignoring it." The Japanese Domei news agency rendered the word to mean "ignore," when the intended meaning was the former. Possibly as a result of a misinterpretation, Harry Truman on August 6, 1945 ordered an atomic bomb which killed over 90,000 people to be dropped on Hiroshima. On August 9th, over 40,000 Japanese died when a second A-bomb was dropped on Nagasaki.

No wonder the Italians say *traduttore-traditore,* "a translator is a traitor."

Replace the following *faux amis* with the correct English meaning. The first letter of each right English meaning has been provided.

1. abusif	Wrong-abusive	Right-e____ OR i____
2. avertissement	Wrong-advertisement	Right-w____
3. éventuel	Wrong-eventual	Right-p____
4. incohérent	Wrong-incoherent	Right-i____
5. pétulant	Wrong-petulant	Right-l____
6. truculent	Wrong-truculent	Right-r____
7. décevoir	Wrong-decieve	Right-d____
8. prétendre	Wrong-pretend	Right-c____
9. phrase	Wrong-phrase	Right-s____
10. sensible	Wrong-sensible	Right-s_____

16

YOU CAN'T TRUST ANYBODY
OVER OR UNDER THIRTY NOT TO
MISQUOTE

WHO ORIGINATED the following expressions?
  a) Any man who hates dogs and children can't be all bad.
  b) If you can't stand the heat, get out of the kitchen.
  c) Let them eat cake. *(Qu'ils mangent de la brioche.)*

If your answers were a) W.C. Fields; b) Harry Truman; c) Marie Antoinette you are wrong on all counts.

The first statement in the mini-quiz was not made by W.C. Fields, but was said about him by writer Leo Rosten when he introduced the comedian at a banquet in 1939. Rosten himself didn't coin the phrase. The expression was hatched in an elevator in 1930 and its progenitor was Byron Darnton, a reporter for the *New York Times*. "If you can't stand the heat, get out of the kitchen" was said by Harry Truman but it was an expression he borrowed from his friend Harry Vaughan. Marie Antoinette never said "let them eat cake." It may have been spoken by a Duchess of Tuscany in 1760 and attributed to the soon-to-be-headless Queen to discredit her.

According to Ralph Keyes in *Nice Guys Finish Seventh* (Collins, 1992), "misquotes drive out real quotes." This takes two main forms: 1) having the right words attributed to the wrong person; 2) having the proper attribution but the wrong words.

It offends our sense of propriety that relative nebbishes (like ourselves) are capable of words that may earn a soupçon of immortality. We'd much rather believe that when something memorable is said, it was pronounced by someone who has enjoyed more than fifteen minutes of fame. For example, the expression "You can't trust anyone over thirty" is usually attributed to either Jerry Rubin or Abbie Hoffman, both noted sixties dissidents. The expression was, in fact, originated by Berkeley dissident Mark Weinberg. Remember Mark Weinberg? That's the point. It seems more fitting that such a symbolic statement be spoken by some counter-cultural icon than by an unknown.

Famous people usually get the credit from the nameless masses for the witticisms they proclaim. Radical feminist Florynce Kennedy is cited as the originator of "If men could get pregnant, abortion would be a sacrament." A decade after this epiphany was attributed to Kennedy, Gloria Steinem revealed that its author was an elderly woman cab driver who carted Ms Steinem and Ms Kennedy through the streets of Boston. This process is not new. Many quotes attributed to Shakespeare were spoken first by others. The Bard is credited with having originated the expression "it's all Greek to me," whereas it was actually used in a play by John Gascoigne twenty years earler.

Even the famous can be bumped off the attribution list if it is deemed that one more famous should get the glory. Shakespeare is usually seen as the creator of "All that glisters is not gold," whereas the maxim was coined by Chaucer more than two hundred years earlier.

Another axiom of quotations is that they will always be shortened. Take the saying attributed to Edmund Burke, "The only thing necessary for the triumph of evil is for good men to do nothing." Burke never said this. The preface to *Bartlett's Familiar Quotations* (fifteenth edition) believes it is a paraphrase of Burke's "When bad men combine, the good must associate; else they will fall one by one, an unpitied sacrifice in a contemptible struggle." The preface states that "whatever the credit, it is the shorter version that will continue to be quoted, you may be assured."

First-century Roman poet Lucan wrote that "pygmies placed on the shoulders of giants see more than the giants themselves." Fifth-century Roman grammarian Prescian, and later both Isaac Newton and Robert Burton, expressed statements very similiar to Lucan's. It is a rare thought that hasn't found previous expression. For example, Franklin Roosevelt's immortal line "The only thing we have to fear is fear itself" took the following earlier forms: "The thing of which I have most fear is fear" (Montaigne, 1580); "Nothing is terrible except fear itself" (Francis Bacon, 1623); "The only thing I am afraid of is fear" (Duke of Wellington, 1832); and "Nothing is so much to be feared as fear" (Thoreau, 1851). Yet we cannot say that Montaigne should "get credit" for the saying, his being the earliest in time. For in Proverbs 3:25, the similar thought, "be not afraid of sudden fear," is expressed.

Sometimes a quote is altered to give it a more universal message. Nice guys didn't finish last in Leo Durocher's famous quote—they finished seventh. This referred to the lowly standing of the "nice" New York Giants, rivals of Durocher's 1946 Brooklyn Dodgers. "Seventh" doesn't resonate the way "last" does, so the expression was altered.

Keyes points out that the prevalence of misquotes has not abated, notwithstanding the greater ability of technology to help record things accurately. Misquotes occur because we hear what and by whom we want to hear something said. And you can misquote me on that.

Replace the following misquoted segments (in italics) with the original version.

1. "Play it *again, Sam*." (Humphrey Bogart in "Casablanca")
2. "I have nothing to offer but *blood, sweat and tears*." (Winston Churchill)
3. "Birds of a feather *flock* together." (Robert Burton)
4. "Ask me no questions, and I'll tell you no *lies*." (Isaac Watts)
5. "One good turn *deserves* another." (John Heywood)
6. "There's safety in *numbers*." (Proverbs)
7. "*He* who hesitates is lost." (Joseph Addison)

17

GOOD GRIEF!

OXYMORA CAN BE REAL MAGIC!

AN OXYMORON IS:

a) a particularly stupid bovine creature
b) an addict to the skin medicine *Oxy-5* or *Oxy-10*
c) a combination of contradictory or incongruous words
d) *Sovereignty-Association* and/or *Progressive Conservative*

The correct answers are c & d. Of course, after the last federal election when the Tories self-destructed, it has become a matter of conjecture whether the P.C.s can be characterized without the "oxy" part of oxymoron.

The word oxymoron is itself oxymoronic. It derives from two contradictory Greek roots: *oxys,* meaning "keen," and *moros,* meaning "foolish." Lest any sophomore think he has gained status now that he is no longer a freshman, he should realize that as a sophomore he is an oxymoronic "wise fool," a collegiate "idiot savant."

My *Oxford English Dictionary* (second edition) defines oxymoron as "A rhetorical figure whereby contradictory or incongruous terms are conjoined so as to give point to the statement or expression; an expression in its superficial or literal meaning self-contradictory or absurd, but involving a point." The majority of oxymora like "jumbo shrimp," "divorce court," "loose tights," "legal brief," "even odds," "civil war" or "pretty ugly," fall within the "superficial" ranks of oxymora. They depend on a play of words to create the supposed contradiction. For example, in the cases of "jumbo shrimp" and "divorce court" it is the double meanings of the words "shrimp" and "court" that create the oxymora.

Another class of oxymora involves terms which are mutually exclusive by nature. Oxymora in this category include "guest host," "slightly pregnant," "bittersweet," "intimate strangers," "down escalator," "good grief," "pure garbage," "environmental sovereignty," "real magic," "recorded live," "deliberate speed," "very unique," "eloquent silence" and "thundering silence."

Many oxymora depend on point of view, such as "safe sex," "military intelligence," "student athlete," "friendly fire," "political science," "Christian Science," "benevolent despot," "Passover food," "rap music," "polite Parisian," "educational TV," "business ethics" and "peace offensive." As one can see, however, the line between true oxymora and judgemental ones is a bit hazy.

Some of the most lyrical oxymora have been coined by literary giants. In Richard Lederer's book *Crazy English,* he lists some of the literary contributions to oxymora. They include Tennyson's "falsely true," Shakespeare's "sweet sorrow," Hemingway's "scalding coolness," Chaucer's "hateful good," Spenser's "proud humility" and Milton's "darkness visible." Tennyson's "falsely true" oxymoron is part of a two line oxymoron trilogy from *Idylls of the King* which reads as follows:

His honour rooted in dishonour stood,
And faith unfaithful kept him falsely true.

The "sweet sorrow" oxymoron voiced by Juliet when she parts from Romeo is perhaps the most quoted English oxymoron. Romeo, however, probably holds the Guinness record for most oxymora in a short space when he confides to his friend Benvolio:

O brawling love! O loving hate!
O anything of nothing first create!

O heavy lightness! serious vanity!
Misshapen chaos of well-seeming forms!
Feather of lead, bright smoke, cold fire, sick health!
Still-waking sleep, that is not what it is!
This love feel I, that feel no love in this.

William Styron borrows John Milton's "darkness visible" as the title of his book on his battle with depression. He characterizes the term depression as a "wimp of a word" that doesn't convey the anguish and powerlessness of the sufferer. Substitutes like "melancholia," "blues," or "lowness" are not an improvement. "Darkness visible" is an example of how an oxymoron can sometimes communicate better than an individual word.

The comedian Yvon Deschamps once said only half-jokingly that what Quebecers want is "an independent Quebec in a united Canada." Judging by the number of institutional oxymora in Canada, I suspect that this blending of polarities is not unique to Quebec. To create oxymoronic symmetry in Parliament with the P.C.s, the Liberals should be redubbed the Reactionary Liberals and the Reform Party should be known as Status Quo Reform. The greatest political oxymoron, however, is the Bloc Quebecois, "Her Majesty's Loyal Opposition." Other Canadian oxymora include "postal service," "negative growth," "decentralized federalism," "Hydro-Québec power," "deflated inflation," "political promises," "lost leaders," "intense apathy" about our "lost leaders" because it's the "same difference;" "fish farms," "justified paranoia" over the economy; and (since the use of the Notwithstanding Clause) the "Supreme Court" of Canada. Hockey oxymora include "offensive defenceman," "plus minus," and "good penalty."

What oxymora loom on the horizon? On the Canadian political front, "proportional asymmetry" could be the next oxymoronic superstar. Unfortunately, "tax-free" is one that is not likely to emerge—that would require a "minor miracle." With the meaning of the word "attitude" mutating from a neutral to a pejorative sense, I'm "99% sure" that one oxymoron to look for is "good attitude"—and that's a "firm maybe."

Complete the following phrases to create oxymora.

1. term for vampires   living _____
2. fill-in for Letterman   guest _____
3. novel by Nabokov   Pale _____
4. Bermudas   long _____
5. pacific overture   peace _____
6. quasi-braking procedure   rolling _____
7. Charlie Brown's expression   good _____
8. boxer of 175 lbs.   light _____
9. Simon & Garfunkle song   Sounds of _____
10. Schwarzenegger flick   True _____

18

MRS. MALAPROP
LIVES ON IN NORTH AMERICAN
POLITICIANS

O NE REASON GIVEN for the defeat of the Bush-Quayle ticket in 1992 was its inability to communicate with the electorate. Bush admitted that "fluency in English is something that I'm not accused of." In 1992, George Bush told a crowd of 15,000 in Ridgefield, New Jersey how much he "appreciated their *recession.*" This statement was topped by Dan Quayle in 1991 who told a gathering that "Republicans understood the importance of *bondage* between mother and child."

In *Canadian Political Babble,* author David Olive gives us some tarnished gems from Canadian politicians in his "metaphorically challenged" section. John Kushner, a Calgary city councillor, told a colleague "don't get your *dandruff* up;" former Toronto mayor Allan Lamport said "I deny the allegation, and I deny the *allega-tors;*" one-time premier of Saskatchewan Allan Blakeney revealed that "all the problems of Saskatchewan are *soluble;*" and when he was but a mere M.P., Fisheries Minister Saint Brian-of-the-Turbot Tobin gave us "Brian Mulroney has left Canada a veritable tower of *Babylon.*"

All our not-so-silver-tongued politicians have committed mala-props. The term derives from Mrs. Malaprop (*mal a propos,* "inap-propriate" in French) a character in Richard Sheridan's 1775 play

The Rivals, who has a penchant for this type of gaffe. She declares one man to be the "very *pineapple* of politeness."

Prior to Sheridan's unveiling Mrs. Malaprop, the term "slip-slop" was used to designate this type of linguistic snafu. Again, we have a literary origin. In Henry Fielding's 1742 novel *Joseph Andrews,* the character Mrs. Slipslop is prone to statements like "When he's had one drink he gets all *erotic*"—meaning erratic. Also, in Tobias Smollett's 1771 novel *Humphry Clinker,* the character Mrs. Winifred Jenkins also commits malaproprian errors. The concept, however, was not an eighteenth-century invention. Shakespeare's comedies employ characters who stretch for a word but only reach a reasonable facsimile. In *Much Ado About Nothing,* Dogberry asks "who think you the most desertless man to be constable?" substituting *"desertless"* for "deserving." Other gaffes in the play include confusing "sensible" with "senseless," "comprehend" with "apprehend," and "suspicious" with "auspicious."

A contemporary Lear, Norman Lear, created a modern Mrs. Malaprop. Archie Bunker of *All In The Family* fame told his wife Edith that if she was experiencing "minstrel" pains while "administrating" she should see the "groinecologist." Gilda Radner on *Saturday Night Live* played a character, Emily Litella, who wondered why people worried about "violins" on television, "jewellery" in the Soviet Union and endangered "feces." When her *faux pas* were exposed her weak rejoinder was "never mind."

The Oxford Companion to the English Language dichotomizes between "classic malapropisms, in which the mistakes are due to ignorance," as with Mrs. Malaprop, and cases when the speaker has inadvertently replaced the intended word by another. The confusibles have similar rhythms, like magician/musician, anecdote/antidote, and—giving Bush the benefit of the doubt—recession/reception.

The humour in malaprops lies in the listener's awareness of the mistake and the speaker's ingenuousness. Malaprops make us feel superior, for *we* wouldn't commit such a gaffe—or would we? It also helps if the replaced word lends a certain irony to the statement, like replacing "bonding" with "bondage," or "monogamy" with "monotony." It is the very artlessness of malaprops that makes them endearing. And aside from the joy of hearing someone screw up, malaprops are entertaining because they reveal hidden connections between words.

In any field where one is exposed to unfamiliar words, substitutions are likely to occur. The field of history is a fertile breeding ground for malaprops. From Richard Lederer's *Anguished English* and *More Anguished English* I have culled the following actual malaprops committed by history students. Restore history by changing the italicized words to the intended words.

1. Moses went up Mount *Cyanide* for the Ten Commandments but died before he reached *Canada*.

2. In Ancient Egypt people wrote in *hydraulics*.

3. King David defeated the *Finkelsteins*.

4. The Great Wall of China was built to keep out the *Mongrels*.

5. The Ancient Greeks built the *Apocalypse*.

6. Socrates died from an overdose of *wedlock*.

7. Pompeii was destroyed by an overflow of saliva from Mount *Vatican*.

8. Roman women built fires in their *brassieres*.

9. In the Middle Ages many people died from the *bluebonnet* plague.

10. Queen Elizabeth's navy defeated the Spanish *armadillo*.

11. Sir Francis Drake *circumcized* the world with a 100-foot clipper.

12. Cervantes wrote *Donkey Hote*.

13. Johann Bach practised on an old *spinster* in his attic.

19

LE PÈRE DE MARIE
EST LE MAIRE DE PARIS

B EHIND EVERY successful eponym there is a person. "Sandwich" originated with the Earl of Sandwich, "chauvinism" with a jingoistic Napoleonic soldier named Nicholas Chauvin, "crap" with Thomas Crapper, the inventor of the modern flush toilet, and "spoonerism" owes its existence to the hero of this chapter, Reverend William Archibald Spooner.

The Reverend Spooner was Warden of New College in Oxford between 1903 and 1924. He was a highly respected administrator responsible for many reforms, but history has been unkind to the dear Reverend. He is not remembered for his forward thinking but for his metatheses, linguistic reversals, which have come to be called "spoonerisms."

Spooner once referred to the hymn *Conquering Kings Their Titles Take* as "kinkering congs," and introduced Dr. Childe's friend as "Dr. Friend's child." The reversals were not limited to words. At a dinner party he upset a salt container and then poured red wine on the salt. One might say that in both words and deeds he "put the heart before the course."

There are not many documented gaffes but this did not stop his supposed bloopers from becoming the stuff of legend to sophomoric Oxonians. During a wedding at which he officiated he supposedly blathered "if anyone present knows why this couple shouldn't be joyfully loined together" and later "it is kisstomary to cuss the bride." Other alleged howlers include:

I have in my bosom a half-warmed fish.

A toast which needs no commendation from me—our queer Dean.

The Lord is a shoving leopard.

You are occupewing the wrong pie. May I sew you to another sheet?

Angry at a student, Spooner is alleged to have declaimed, "You have hissed all my mystery lectures and tasted two worms. I saw you fight a liar. Pack up your rags and bugs, and leave immediately by the town drain."

What causes accidental linguistic gaffes? Sigmund Freud viewed these slips of the tongue as symptomatic of unconscious forces or mental conflict deep in the psyche. Freud's interpretation doesn't account for the majority of gaffes, which are not particularly dramatic, such as saying "right lane" instead of "light rain." More plausible is the explanation provided by Professor Laurence Goldstein. He believes the errors are "due to interference of the preparatory processing of sounds soon to be produced. . . . We appear to think ahead to the sounds we shall need to make. . . ."

Must the tips of the slung be accidental? Lot on your knife! Walter Redfern states in his book *Puns* that "All humour, and much intelligence, entails an ability to think on two planes at once." Spoonerisms have the added feature over regular puns of having not just one but two wordplays. According to Don Hauptman in *Cruel And Unusual Puns,* the "humour lies in the perceived incongruity or absurdity between two incompatible frames of reference." He believes spoonerisms' appeal lies in the mind's seeking symmetry and balance. "In perceiving both sides of the equation, there is a sense of completion or resolution."

Take for example the joke: "What's the difference between a rooster and a lawyer? The rooster clucks defiance. . . ." The joke

only works if the listener can make the correct linguistic trans-
posal and share in the satisfaction. The only one not amused is
the attorney.

One popular form of spooneristic pun is the "shaggy dog"
story. An example of such is the following tale: "Sir Lancelot was
riding back to Camelot on a stormy night when his horse tumbled
and broke a leg. He noticed a peasant's house and while knocking
loudly on the door he shouted, "I must get back to the Round
Table. Give me a horse!" The peasant answered, "Sire, we have no
horse but only a German Shepherd." Lancelot replied, "I have no
choice. Saddle up your cur and I'll ride him home." The peasant
retorted, "Sire, I wouldn't send a knight out on a dog like this."

Don Hauptman opens a chapter on sexual spoonerisms, "If
you like erotic humour . . . this is your ducky lay!" English has so
many words with multiple meanings that the most innocuous
comment can result in a double entendre. Hauptman proposes
the following spooneristic title for a low brow raunchy soap opera,
"Lays of our Dives."

In spite of the endless possibilities, English must take a back
seat to French in bawdy word transposals. *Contrèpeterie*, as it is
called in French, goes back to the twelfth century. *Contrepèts* need
not be lewd, but the most memorable ones are lusty. Rabelais is
considered to be the father of the coarse variety. Here are some
examples of Rabelaisian *contrepet*:

— *Femme folle à la Messe/molle à la fesse.* (The woman is crazy in
church/she has a soft ass.)
— *Une pierre fine/fière pine.* (A fine jewel/a proud penis.)
— *Les laborieuses populations du Cap/copulations du Pape.* (The
laborious populations of the Cape/the painstaking copulations of
the Pope.)
— *Les fables de la comtesse/les fesses de la comptable.* (The fables of
the countess/the asses of the accountant.)
— *Pour entrer aux Carmélites, il faut savoir utiliser le mot de
guichet/le godemiché* (To enter the Carmelite nunnery one has to
know how to use the password/the dildo.)

– *Les Anglaises aiment le tennis en pension/le penis en tension.*
(English girls at boarding schools like tennis/erect penises.)

Now that spoonerisms have captured your "marts and hinds," try making up your own. You have nothing to "choose but your lanes" and you can't "feel the beating" of the "shaming of the true." Beware, *je vous en prie*, or is that *je vous y prends?* For they are addictive. Beware of "geeks bearing grifts." Leave "no tern unstoned," I mean "no Stern untoned," I mean, "no stone unturned." After all, "a dirty mind is a horrible thing to waste" or is that "a horrible waist is a dirty thing to mind" or . . . .

Create spoonerisms from the following definitions.

1. A description of one of the joys of S & M: It's fun to be ____.

2. Trying to embarrass the faithful: Shaming ___ ___ ___.

3. The privilege of ursine protection: The right to ___ ___.

4. The bane of those who prefer booze to labour: Work is the curse of the ___ ____.

5. Description of Patrick Roy throwing a party?: goalie _____.

6. Chinese regulation (spoonerism to DeNiro flick): Beijing ___.

7. Alcoholic's refrain: "I'd rather have a bottle in front of me than have a _____ ____."

8. Definition of alcoholism: The wrath of _____.

9. To make fun of a hawk: To ____ a _____ bird.

10. Immunity to torture?: Can't feel the _____.

20

IT ISN'T A-OK
IN MANY PARTS OF THE WORLD

I N THE 1950's, then-Vice President Richard Nixon went on a
goodwill tour of Central America. He alighted from his plane
and flashed the "A-OK" sign (formed by making a circle with the
thumb and forefinger with the other three fingers extended
upward) to the waiting crowd who, instead of welcoming him,
booed vigorously. In a joint venture of German and American
engineers, a German asked his American counterpart if he had
completed a procedure properly. When the American responded
with the aforementioned OK sign, the German stormed out of the
room.

Why did the OK signs elicit such anger? In Latin America,
Nixon's gesture suggested a carnal act of great agility whereas to
the German it meant "You jerk!"

These anecdotes are culled from *Gestures: The Dos and Taboos
of Body Language Around the World* (Wiley, 1991) by Roger E. Axtell.
Although our species may be defined by its ability to communicate verbally, 60% of all human communication is non-verbal.
Words may be the vehicle for ideas but without gestures those
ideas would be cold and mechanical. Gestures can serve as a communication shortcut. They are more emphatic than punctuation
or the stressing of words in bold-face or italics. Social scientist

Flora Davis says, "They are like the maestro's baton to each musician in the ensemble." To communicate an emotional state, gestures are more reliable than words. Our unawareness, in many instances, of our gestures, makes them all the more revealing. Gestures can indeed speak louder than words. Shakespeare wrote in *The Winter's Tale,* "There was speech in their dumbness, language in their every gesture."

According to linguist Mario Pei, humans are capable of making 760,000 distinct gestures. Some of them are made with parts of the body one wouldn't expect. The "nose tap" in England is a call for confidentiality, whereas in Italy it is a way of saying "take care." In Thailand, pointing with your toes is considered insulting, especially if you have the flexibilty to aim them at someone's head. The "cheek screw," in which a forefinger is rotated into the cheek, has many meanings: in Italy, praise; in Germany, craziness; and in Spain, effeminacy.

One would think that the nodding of the head up and down, meaning "yes," and the shaking of it from side to side to mean "no" would be universal. Think again. In Bulgaria, Turkey, and the former Yugoslavia, you nod for "no" and shake for "yes." In parts of Greece there are even nuances to this arrangement. You indicate "no" by tipping your head back abruptly while raising your eyebrows, and you say "yes" by dropping the chin three times. Got it?

The handshake on the White House lawn between Arafat and Rabin was the defining image of the momentous Palestinian-Israeli peace accord. Because it occurred publicly, the clasping of hands of formerly implacable foes, although tentative, was a symbol of mutual recognition. It is based on this recognition that the embryonic hope for peace rests. Surprisingly, the handshake, which has become the *lingua franca* of greetings, is only two hundred years old. Its original function, like an embrace or the Indian *namaste* (hands in a praying position), is to demonstrate an absence of weapons. Shaking of hands may now be universal, but its mode is not. While a firm shake is in order in North America and Europe, a gentle grasp is preferred in the Middle East and the Orient. Too firm a clasp may be construed as aggression. Axtell tells us that Prince Charles, whom he describes as a "connoisseur of greetings," has complained about the finger-crunching variety employed by Texans. Who shakes whom also varies considerably. Women and children will initiate handshakes in Northern Europe but are unlikely to do so in the Far East. In Islamic countries, it is taboo for an unrelated man to touch a woman and thus offering one's hand to a woman may be ill-advised.

Communication is not only effected by one's body but also by its surrounding space. This "bubble of personal space," as it is sometimes referred to, represents the personal space we feel we own. The size of the bubble varies greatly in different cultures. In North America and Northern Europe the safety zone extends from twelve to fifteen inches, so the distance between two people talking will be between twenty-four and thirty inches. The Japanese prefer even more personal space. When very close quarters are unavoidable, as in a subway, the Japanese will deny the proximity by not making eye contact.

Conversely, the bubbles in Latin America and the Middle East hardly exist at all. When the twain meet between different cultures this can lead to a dance called the "conversational tango." Here's how the choreography works. A Canadian talking to an Abu Dhabian will probably retreat in response to his partner's proximity. The latter, feeling the Canadian is slipping away from him, will probably move a step forward to narrow the gap. Sometimes the dance will only end when the back-pedalling Canadian is backed into a corner.

21

SUPPORTING YOUR FOOTBALL
TEAM IN ITALY CAN BE DANGEROUS
TO YOUR HEALTH

L INGUIST EDWARD SAPIR defined non-verbal communication as the "elaborate and secret code that is written nowhere, known by none, and understood by all." He should have added to the end of the sentence the clause *"members of a particular culture."* For if you don't understand the rudimentary gestures of a society, you'll find it difficult to communicate effectively, notwithstanding some fluency in the particular language.

According to Roger Axtell, author of *Gestures,* gestures that we use every day might be considered insulting somewhere in the world. If you're thumbing a ride in Nigeria, expect a hostile reaction because the thumb position is regarded as obscene. The same gesture in Turkey might be seen as an invitation to a same-sex liaison.

When I grew up, everyone knew that the sign made with the second and fifth fingers was a challenge towards the veracity of someone's position, i.e, the "bullshit" sign. For University of Texas football fans it is known as the "hook 'em horns" sign and is flashed as a signal of support for their team, the Longhorns. This sign in Italy has a totally different meaning and Axtell relates how this led to an international incident. Some American soldiers from Texas met some fellow Texans in a bar and they began bonding with "hook 'em horns" signs. Before they knew it, they were jostled by angry Italian patrons and waiters and a brawl ensued. Why? Because for Italian men this sign was one of mockery. It signified that they were being cuckolded, i.e., that their wives were being unfaithful.

When shopping in the Plaka in Athens, a tourist might extend his palm outward in an effort to stop the come-on of an aggressive street vendor. Again, this gesture may offend. It is known as the *moutza,* and it dates back to ancient Greece, when fecal matter was thrown at war prisoners. In parts of West Africa this same gesture implies that the identity of your father is open-ended.

Don't think that you only have to concern yourself with movements of the upper body. In many parts of the Middle and Far East, showing the soles of your shoes is deemed offensive. To complicate matters, in some countries it is customary to converse while sitting on cushions on the floor. For non-contortionist Westerners this makes sole pointing highly problematic.

Even beckoning a waiter can be confounding. The North American habit of lifting an arm with an extended index finger would not be proper in Japan, where any finger pointing is looked at askance. In Germany, if you beckon a waiter with *two* uplifted fingers and ask for some water, you're liable to get *two* glasses of water. Axtell tells us that in Latin America and Europe the definitive beckoning gesture is "to extend the arm, hand out, palm down, and then make a scratching motion of your fingers." Insulting someone because of an ignorance of local gestures is regrettable. Conversely, an intended salvo that misses the mark can be maddening. In England, the "V for victory" sign, immortalized by Winston Churchill and adopted by peaceniks, is only valid in the palm-outward position. When the palm is in the inward position, the gesture acquires an obscene meaning. This dichotomy, however, does not transcend the British Isles. Desmond Morris, in *Manwatching,* relates that "Englishmen when travelling abroad have often been nonplussed at the total failure of this sign (palm inward) when directed, say, towards an Italian driver."

Chances are that the Italian motorist will just wave and smile, leaving the Brit in an apoplectic state.

After being cut off while driving, my gesture of choice is the twirling of the forefinger around my temple to denote the mentally-challenged nature of my antagonist. If I repeated this gesture in Argentina it would be interpreted as meaning "you have a telephone call." I wouldn't have to worry about any misinterpretation in Germany. This gesture is regarded as so rude that motorists have been arrested for twirling while driving.

If you're making a business trip to Japan, Axtell recommends wearing glistening shoes because you'll be looking at them often while bowing. You won't elicit a samurai response if you don't bow, but a slight bow shows respect for their customs. Knowing the rank of those you're meeting is important, because the person of lower rank is expected to bow first and lower.

Attitudes towards touching vary widely throughout the world. In some Arab countries it is common for men to hold hands. Doing so upon meeting a stranger is a token of friendship. Jerking your hand away in this situation may be construed as hostile. Conversely, placing your arm around a Japanese business associate may be deemed to be a space invasion, and thus rude.

In a multicultural society, realizing that gestures are culturally based can avoid misunderstandings. A Korean storekeeper who doesn't make eye contact with you and avoids putting the change in your hand is not being unfriendly. In his culture, to do otherwise would be impolite.

One shouldn't regard knowledge of gestures as only a means of avoiding embarrassment. Desmond Morris states in his politically-incorrectly titled book *Manwatching* that "wherever people behave, there the man-watcher has something to learn about his fellow-man and, ultimately, about himself."

PART IV

LANGUAGE AT PLAY

Playing with language is instinctive. Even before mastering grammar, we play with the sounds of language. But wordplay is seen by some as an activity that non-frivolous adults should forego. This is unfortunate, since wordplay is both a joy and a learning tool. It stands to reason that a student who enjoys playing with words will be a motivated reader. Indeed, an indictment against wordplay is tantamount to an indictment against literature. For isn't poetry essentially a playing with words in an attempt to create symmetry?

Sixteenth-century theologian Desiderius Erasmus stated, "Nothing is more foolish than to talk of frivolous things seriously; but nothing is wittier than to make frivolities serve various ends."

22

THE PUN IS MIGHTIER
THAN THE SWORD

To pun or not to pun? Puns have been much maligned by a host of writers and thinkers. Freud described puns as "cheap," Oliver Wendell Holmes assailed them as "verbicide," and Ambrose Bierce in his *Devil's Dictionary* defined a pun as "a form of wit to which wise men stoop and fools aspire." Puns, however, have had their defenders. Three hundred years ago Henry Erskine countered John Dennis' statement that "a pun is the lowest form of wit" by adding that "it is therefore the foundation of all wit." Pundit Oscar Levant said that it is the "lowest form of humour—when you didn't think of it first." Canadian John S. Crosbie, founder of the International Save the Pun Foundation, opines that one should challenge the claim that puns are the lowest form of humour by declaring that "poetry is verse."

Samuel Beckett, in his novel *Murphy*, states that "in the beginning was the pun," to which can be added that God said "let there be light," for it had fewer calories yet tasted great.

Punning would appear to be a fixture of language through the ages. R. Blyth in *Oriental Humour* states that in "ancient Sanskrit literature there is an almost unbelievable amount of punning. Puns were the delight of a small number of great men with unsolemn minds." In Homer's *Odyssey*, Odysseus introduces himself to the Cyclops Polyphemus as Outis, which means "no man" in Greek. Odysseus attacks the giant, who calls for reinforcement from his fellow monsters, with the plea "no man is killing me!" Naturally, no one rushes to his aid, proving that the pun is indeed mightier than the sword. Cicero was another habitual punster. When a man ploughed up the burial ground of his father, Cicero couldn't resist interjecting, *"Hoc est vere colere monumentum patris"* (this is truly to cultivate a father's memory).

In the Bible there are many puns on names. In Hebrew, *"adamah"* means ground and *"edom"* means red. The name Adam may derive from the red earth whence he came. The name Jacob is derived from the word for heel, because he held onto the heel of his older twin brother Esau at birth. The best known Biblical pun is by Jesus in Matthew 16:18: "thou art Peter (Greek, Petros), and upon this rock (Greek, Petra) I will build my Church." Pope Gregory, guardian of the Rock, punned when he stated that English slaves were *"Non Angli, sed angeli"* (not Anglos, but angels).

The heyday of English language puns was the Elizabethan era. Wordplay was enjoyed by all strata of society. The creation of puns was facilitated by the many recent borrowings from the Romance languages. This created a wealth of homonyms, the building blocks of puns. Queen Elizabeth herself punned doubly when she declared: "You may be burly, my Lord of Burleigh, but ye shall make less stir in my realm than the Lord of Leicester." Most Elizabethan writers dabbled in puns. Their ranks included poets John Donne and Andrew Marvell, and virtually all the playwrights, including Shakespeare.

Victor Margolin declares that "in the art of punning, Shakespeare was great shakes and without peer." Molly Mahood, in *Shakespeare's Wordplay,* estimates that there are 3000 puns in the Bard's works, with an average of 78 puns per play. Many of these puns occur at climactic moments. After Macbeth has killed the King, Lady Macbeth displays a lucid dispassion when she avers "I'll *gild* the faces of the grooms withal. For it must seem their *guilt.*" In *King Henry IV, Part Two,* when Henry Percy discovers his son Hotspur is slain, he says: "Said he young Harry Percy's spur was cold? Of Hotspur, Coldspur?" In *Romeo and Juliet* the dying Mercutio exits stage left with the vaudevillean pun, "Ask for me tomorrow and you shall find me a grave man." Even noble Hamlet can't resist expiring with the pun "the rest is silence."

Shakespeare's puns can be quite lewd. Some of the bawdiness occurs in seemingly innocuous phrases like "too much of a good thing," spoken by Rosalind to Orlando in *As You Like It*. In Shakespeare's day, "thing" was a common euphemism for genitalia. Some scholars see sexual allusions everywhere. Frankie Rubinstein in *Dictionary of Shakespeare's Sexual Puns* claims that the following words all have sexual connotations: ability, abstinence, abuse, access, accost, achieve and actions. And we're not even halfway through the letter A. In the opening scene of *Julius Caesar* a punning cobbler describes himself as a "surgeon to old shoes; when they are in great danger, I recover them." Rubinstein tells us that in Elizabethan vernacular "surgeon" refers to the treatment of venereal disease, and thus it is not shoes that are being mended, but the bottoms of whores.

For famed lexicographer Samuel Johnson, a pun represented to Shakespeare "the fatal Cleopatra for which he lost the world and was prepared to lose it." Samuel Coleridge disagreed saying "a pun, if congruous with the feeling of a scene is not only allowable . . . but oftentimes the most effective intensives of passions."

But what is art in the Bard's deft hand can be downright maddening when abused by lesser mortals. Oliver Wendell Holmes suggested that killing a punster was warranted if the pun is bad enough. A story is told of a king who decides not to hang his jester if only the fool will forswear puns. The jester responds "no noose is good news," so the King hung him. Yes, many puns are in bad taste, but as Walter Redfern says in *Puns,* "bad taste is where we mostly live . . . and puns are not a device, an instrument to be grasped or spat upon but a whole way of feeling, seeing, thinking and expressing."

23

PUNUPMANSHIP

W HAT MAKES A GOOD PUN? Henry Fowler in his *Dictionary of Modern English Usage* makes the issue sound downright empirical: "Puns are good, bad and indifferent, and only those who lack the wit to make them are unaware of the fact." I am not a proponent of Fowler's axiom. Puns are like pearls, born out of irritation. I subscribe to Lamb's law. To Charles Lamb, bad was good: "A pun is not bound by the laws which limit nicer wit. It is a pistol let off at the ear, not a feather to tickle the intellect. The puns which are the most entertaining are those which will bear the least analysis."

No doubt Lamb would have liked this groaner: A timid husband is unable to buy his wife's favourite anemones for her birthday and fearfully returns home bearing some greenery. To his surprise she gushes "with fronds like this who needs anemones?"

Here's a brief sampling of puns both sublime and ridiculous from some well-known pundits.

Groucho Marx—Time wounds all heels.

Edgar Bergen—Show me where Stalin's buried and I'll show you a Communist plot.

Max Eastman—One of the advantages of nuclear war is that all men are cremated equal.

Dorothy Parker (asked to give a sentence with the word horticulture)—You can lead a horticulture but you can't make her think.

Milton Berle (definition of a committee)—A group of men who spend hours taking minutes.

Mae West—It's not the men in your life that counts—it's the life in your men.

George S. Kaufman—One man's Mede is another man's Persian.

Oscar Wilde—Working is the curse of the drinking class.

John S. Crosbie—A day without a pun is a day without sunshine; there is gloom for improvement.

H.L. Mencken—Television is like a steak: a medium rarely well done.

Puns are employed as slogans because of their economy. To Polonius' maxim that "brevity is the soul of wit," can be added "and advertising space is costly." The following are signs and slogans that have appeared around the world. Most of them are drawn from Richard Lederer's *Get Thee To a Punnery.*

Beauty Salon—Curl up and dye.

Butcher shop—We will sell no swine before its time.

Plumber—A flush is better than a full house.

Catholic church—Litany candles?

Music shop—Gone Chopin. Bach in a minuet.

Shoe store—Come in and have a fit.

Diaper truck—Rock a dry baby.

Tailor shop—Euripedes-Eumenides.

Puns are more than mere whimsy. They represent our first exposure as children to our folk culture. The earliest joke I remember as a child was the following punnish riddle, "What has four wheels and flies? Answer—a garbage truck." Then there was the following off-colour (by 1950 standards) ditty. "Why do firemen have bigger balls than policemen? Answer—they sell more tickets."

Montreal psychologist Margie Golick, in the introduction to her book *Playing With Words,* tells us that she uses wordplay when working with children with language delays: "Word games . . . further language development. They get children . . . talking and listening, thinking about the form and meaning of words and sentences." Puns also serve an important psychological function as a denial of anxiety. Peter de Vries describes them oxymoronically as the "belligerence of the insecure." Shakespearean characters use puns in this manner, none more so than Hamlet. Mahood in *Shakespeare's Wordplay* says that "at times Hamlet's wordplay does double duty by both masking his hostility towards Claudius and affording him a safety-valve for his bitterness at his mother's guilt."

A pun is a world of possibility. It reshapes the language we use to describe the world and in that sense can be seen as a political gesture, even a revolutionary one. Shared laughter aimed at a common enemy can be a catalyst to audacity. In *Puns*, Redfern quotes Guiraud, who states, "Puns are one of the main weapons of political satire under dictatorships. They flourish during wars of religion, the Revolution, the Occupation and, nearer our time, in most police states." A pun under Brezhnev's USSR regime declared that there was no news in *Pravda* (truth in Russian) and no truth in *Izvestia* (news in Russian). E. Larsen in *Wit as a Weapon* relates the following *Flusterwitze*, or "whispered joke" in Nazi Germany: A German gazes at portraits of Hitler, Goebbels and Göring and wonders, "Should one hang them up or put them against the wall?"

I will leave you to meditate on the following observation by Fred Allen: "Hanging is too good for a man who makes puns. He ought to be drawn and quoted."

Words that sound the same, like bier/beer, but are different in spelling and meaning are called homophones. The beauty shop with the "Curl up and dye" sign is employing a homophonic pun. Figure out the following animal homophones with the clues provided. For example, "Smokey in the nude" would be "bare bear."

1. Female insect relation
2. Insect twitch
3. Entomological power
4. Merit a sea eagle
5. Macho mollusk display
6. Moby Dick's lament
7. Kermit lost his parking spot
8. Spirit of fish
9. Expensive doe
10. Bambi's bread
11. Bullwinkle in a blender
12. Tabloid for antelopes
13. Rabbit fur
14. Fibbin' feline
15. Golf course for wildcats
16. Cat that uses steroids (In Brooklynese)
17. Female horse's French mother
18. Nay a neigh
19. Long-winded pig
20. Irregular simian warrior

24

WE'RE COMPLETELY
SURROUNDED (ON ALL SIDES)
BY PLEONASMS

I N A 1993 INTERVIEW with Hana Gartner, Jean Chretien stated that he was respected by most Quebecers, and that it was only the "intellectual intelligentsia" who disparaged him. I ask you Mr. Chretien, what other type of intelligentsia is there? George Bush probably outdid Chretien in one of his televised debates. He made reference to the "economic economy." Small wonder his economic policies were not too popular with the American populace living in the United States.

These are two of the more egregious examples of redundant language but yea, we are not drowning in a sea of unnecessary words, but in a veritable swamp. Why can't things be merely null, why do they have to be void? If I look in every nook, must I explore every cranny? Must I desist when I cease, abet when I aid, choose when I pick and rave when I rant? Can't I just cease, aid, pick and rant? When we talk about "false pretences," a couple being "joined together," "close proximity," "hating with a passion" and a woman "pregnant with child," I ask, what are the alternatives?

Have you ever seen a young geezer, a cold water heater, a non-living survivor, or a non-lazy bum? I've smelled, with my own nose, different bouquets but the only type I've ever seen, with my own eyes, is the flowery variety.

Am I paranoid, or is there some secret of time only I can't intuit? I first became suspicious when Dan Quayle said, "I have made good judgements in the future." Then I started wondering why people referred to "future plans," a "whole future in front of them" or "advance warning." This implies there are alternatives like past plans and a past future. The past is equally beguiling. Why do we specify "past experience" and "never before?" Aren't all experiences "past?" Why does "before" have to be added to "never?" Is there a dimension called the "never after" of which I'm not aware? I worry when someone tells me the "honest truth," or gives me a "garden salad" to eat, or something "100% pure" to drink. Does that mean that if they tell me only the truth or ply me with a mere salad or a beverage that's only pure I'm in "serious danger?" Do I overexaggerate? I continue to remain in a state of uneasy anxiety.

Mercifully, it takes but a single word to describe verbal redundancy. The term is "pleonasm." It derives from the Latin *pleonasmus* which, in turn, comes from the Greek *pleonasmos* ("moreness"). Antony's line in *Julius Caesar,* "the most unkindest cut of all," is an example of a pleonasm done for effect, as is the biblical "I AM THAT I AM." In any case, Moses wasn't about to accuse the Burning Bush of redundancy.

Most pleonasms, however, are not so stylish and denote only poor form. "Could you repeat that again?" is an example of a commonly used pleonasm. A redundancy can be avoided by saying either "Could you say that again?" or "Could you repeat that?" Don't say "each and every" when "every" suffices, nor say "she is a woman who" when "she is" will do, or use "if and when" when only "if" is required. The word "fact" is a major pleonastic culprit. "In spite of the fact" can be replaced with "though," "owing to the fact" can be reduced to "because," and "unaware of the fact" can be shortened to "unaware that."

Perhaps I'm just an unprogressive conservative who pines for the days when you didn't need to qualify that a gift was free, a victim innocent, a fact true, a record new, and scholarship academic. In the past, one didn't have to specify strictly private or natural grass. Then again, some pleonasms like "cash money" and "disposable garbage" have evolved into possible states of non-redundancy. Some might say that in the past "heterosexual sex" was pleonastic. Unfortunately, a former pleonasm, "healthy tan," has mutated into an oxymoronic state in our ozone-depleted world.

So, who is to blame? As I live and breathe, I think I know the party responsible for our modern orgy of redundacy. J'accuse Raid Bug Repellant. Their slogan read *"Raid kills bugs dead."* To keep pace with this linguistic overkill, other ads stressed products that were "new innovations," "more superior" and "very unique." *McDonald's* isn't content to sell billions of hamburgers. They advertise "billions and billions." And don't think the pleonastic process only flows towards aggrandizement. Isn't a dot miniscule enough? Must we have microdots?

There are times when a pleonasm can be employed successfully for rhetorical effect. Usually, however, unnecessary words suck the juice out of phrases. In *A Dictionary of Modern English Usage,* H.W. Fowler states, "There are many phrases originally put together for the sake of such emphasis, but repeated with less and less effect until they end by boring instead of impressing the hearer. . . . Those who would write vigorously have to . . . unlearn them."

Start unlearning. J. Dansforth Quayle, the man who provided impeachment insurance to George Bush, said in 1989: "If we don't succeed, we run the risk of failure."

N.B. (Making a duplicate copy of this chapter in any shape or form without my express, intended permission, and authorization is totally and utterly allowed, and indeed more preferable than alternate options.)

Many expressions in English are redundant. Fill in the blanks with the word (or words) that express the same thought as its pair.

1. trials & _____
2. intents & _____
3. cease & _____
4. pick & _____
5. over & _____ _____
6. each & _____
7. null & _____
8. safe & _____
9. first & _____

10. ways & _____
11. vim & _____
12. highways & _____
13. lo & _____
14. rack & _____
15. kit & _____
16. prim & _____
17. hue & _____
18. wild & _____

25

PALINDROMES
SEMORDNILAP

M Y *Oxford English Dictionary* (second edition) defines a palindrome as "a word, verse, or sentence that reads the same when the letters composing it are taken in the reverse order." Examples of palindromes are the words *"level"* and *"deified,"* and the sentences *"Sex at noon taxes"* and *"Madam, I'm Adam."*

The word "palindrome" comes from the Greek *palindromos,* which translates as "running back again." It should not be confused with *hippodrome,* which is an arena where horses are, hopefully, running only forward.

Sotades, a Thracian iconoclast, is generally credited with inventing palindromic sentences. This accounts for the palindrome's alternative name, "Sotadics." Sotades, however, burst one balloon too many. He made the mistake of satirizing the Egyptian king Ptolemy II in one of his palindromes. The humourless king didn't appreciate Sotades' wit and had him stuffed inside a lead chest and thrown in the sea.

Perhaps due to Sotades' fate, other palindromists of yore were pen-shy, for few ancient palindromes are still known. One ancient Greek palindrome was sometimes put on fountains. It read *Nispon anomimata mimonan opsin,* which means "Wash the sin as well as the face." Another surviving palindrome was probably a slogan on the business cards of ancient Roman lawyers and an inspiration to Robert Shapiro and Johnny Cochrane. It read *Si nummi immunis,* which translates roughly as "Pay me and I'll get you off."

The majority of palindromes seem to be written in Latin and English but their use is not unknown to other languages. The palindromist Alastair Reid, in his book *Passwords,* written in 1959, quotes palindromes in French, *Eh, ça va, la vache?,* and Spanish, *Dabale arroz a la zorra el abad,* which has something to do with rice, a prostitute and an abbot.

John Taylor is credited with devising the first English palindrome. In his *Nipping or Snipping of Abuses* written in 1614, he confesses palindromically, *"Lewd did I live, & evil I did dwel."* "Dwel" is an old spelling of "dwell" and the use of an ampersand is not totally kosher. Order can be returned to the universe if we rewrite it like this, *"Evil I did dwel; lewd did I live."* One of the best known English palindromes is attributed to an enisled Anglophile Napoleon who is purported to have intoned, *"Able was I ere I saw Elba."* Perhaps inspired by the immortality Napoleon attained by his palindromic lament, twentieth-century politicians have had a penchant for palindromic ejaculations. Curiously, all these utterances are in English. Here is a sampling:

I, man, am regal, a German am I. (Attributed to William II, Emperor of Germany; 1914.)

Ned, rob Borden. (Attributed to Liberal leader Wilfrid Laurier, angry at Prime Minister Borden's plans to institute conscription— suggests to an underling named Ned to mug the P.M.; 1917.)

Jar a tonga; nag not a raj. (Winston Churchill warns Mahatma Gandhi not to oppose British rule in India; 1942.)

Not now! Foe Tibetan ate bite of won ton. (Attributed to Mao Zedong, referring to the Dalai Lama; 1959.)

Did I gag as Mandela totaled name of S.A? Gag I did. (Attributed to South African P.M. Verwoerd, referring to Mandela's denunciation of Apartheid at his trial; 1964.)

Can I attain a C? (Attributed to Prince Charles in his quest for mediocrity while attending Trinity College; 1967.)

In a regal age ran I. (Attributed to the staunch monarchist, Ex
P.M. John Diefenbaker in his memoirs; 1974.)

To last, Carter retracts a lot. (Attributed to Gerald Ford in his
Presidential debate with Jimmy Carter; 1976.)

Doc, note I dissent. A fast never prevents a fatness. I diet on cod.
(Attributed to a recalcitrant John Crosbie objecting to the strict
diet his physician has ordered; 1983.)

A man, a pot age? I, Ronnie, rein Noriega to Panama. (Attributed
to Ronald Reagan; 1986.)

Egad! A red loses older adage. (Attributed to Margaret Thatcher
referring to Gorbachev's reforms; 1988.)

Evil odes or prose do live. (Attributed to Ayatollah Khoumeini
referring to Rushdie's *Satanic Verses;* 1988.)

Did I step on dog poop? God, no pets, I did! (Attributed to V.P. Dan
Quayle while walking on the White House lawn; 1989.)

Poor Dan is in a droop. (Attributed to Mrs. Quayle after the
above incident; 1989.)

Are we not, Rae, near to new era? (Attributed to Audrey
Mclaughlin congratulating Bob Rae on his electoral victory in
Ontario, 1990.)

Drat! Saddam a mad dastard. (Attributed to the Emir of Kuwait,
Sheik Jaber al-Ahmed upon discovering that his country was
being invaded by Iraq; 1990.)

'Mad dash to me, Hebrew snail.' I answer: 'Behemoth Saddam!'
(Attributed to Yitzhak Shamir describing to his analyst his recur-
ring nightmare; 1991.)

No, Rome, moron! (George Bush shows displeasure with his
Veep who goes to Nome, Alaska and misses an important conference in Rome; 1992.)

Sex at noon taxes. (Attributed to Bill Clinton; 1993.)

No, in uneven union! (Attributed to Jacques Parizeau; 1994.)

Figure out the palindromic word or expression with the clues provided.

1. Type of playing field   _ _ v _ _
2. Model of Honda   _ _ v _ _
3. Second largest city in Quebec   _ _ v _ _
4. President of Argentina   _ _ n _ _
5. Tennis star   _ _ l _ _
6. Time of day   _ _ o _
7. brighter   _ _ _ d _ _
8. Inuit canoe   _ _ y _ _
9. Turned into a god   _ _ _ f _ _ _
10. Japanese car   _ _ _ y _ _ _
11. Part that precedes 'or shut up'   _ _ t _ _
12. Grand Prix vehicle   _ _ c _ _ _ _
13. Opposite of push-up   _ _ _ l _ _
14. Napoleon's supposed enisled lament   a _ _ _ _ _ _ _
     _ _ _ _ s _ _ _ _ _ a

26

PROVERBIAL ABUSE

W*ebster's Encyclopedic Unabridged Dictionary's* first definition of the word cliché is a "trite, stereotyped expression; a sentence or phrase, usually expressing a popular or common thought or idea, that has lost originality, ingenuity, and impact by long overuse, as 'sadder but wiser,' or 'strong as an ox'." The key word in this definition to the origin of the word cliché is *"stereotype." Cliché* is actually the past participle of the French word *clicher,* which means "to stereotype." A cliché was a cast, or "dab," applied especially to a metal stereotype of a wood-engraving used for printing. Printers in early English type foundries called the process "dabbing." The verb *clicher* was itself an adaptation of the verb *cliquer,* which means "to click." Thus, there is an onomatopoeic origin to the word cliché, for as the mold fell into its hot bath it made a clicking sound.

According to the *Oxford English Dictionary* (second edition), Charles Darwin in 1868 uses the word in the original sense when he writes in *Life III,* "Engelman has . . . offered me clichés of the woodcuts." The modern sense of cliché was first used in 1892 by A. Lang in *Longman's Magazine:* "They have the hatred of clichés and commonplace, of the outworn phrase of clashing consonants." By 1895, the word's pejorative connotation is extended when the *Westminster Gazette* reports, "The farcical American woman who 'wakes everybody up' with her bounding vulgarities is rapidly becoming a cliché both on the stage and in fiction."

Clichés have become an easy target for writers on language. Donna Woolfolk Cross in her book *Word Abuse* writes, "Clichés don't have to make a great deal of sense. Whether they do or not, people keep using them. A person who wouldn't dream of using someone else's toothbrush will feel not a qualm about using someone else's tired expression." This position, I believe, is too harsh because sometimes using a cliché is the best form of expression. The cliché may be overused but because it is common it is likely to be understood. Philip Howard, in *The State of the Language,* states, "Poets and philosophers mint brand new language. The rest of us have to make do with the common currency that passes ceaselessly from hand to eye and mouth to ear. The most overworked cliché is better than an extravagant phrase that does not come off."

There is one cliché, however, that I would like to see retired. Politicians, in particular, like the cliché, "Don't throw out the baby with the bathwater." What sort of deranged mind would even contemplate this in the first place? Clichés tend to use metaphors that are no longer pertinent to modern urban life. I, for one, have never inspected a molehill, or counted chickens either before or after they're hatched. I refuse to grab a bull by any part of its anatomy. I can never remember if the cart goes before the horse, or if the horse goes before the cart. Come to think of it, I've never even let a cat out of a bag.

I suspect there are other befuddled souls who share my problem. As Sam Goldwyn once said, "Let's have some new clichés." I, therefore, offer the following cliché updates:

Old Expression	*New Expression*
Time is money.	Time is a credit card.
Out of the frying pan into the fire.	Out of the Cuisinart, into the microwave.

If you can't stand the heat, get
   out of the kitchen.

If you can't stand your
   kitchen, renovate.

All that glitters is not gold.

All that glitters isn't sequin.

You can lead a horse to water,
   but you can't make
   him drink.

You can take a Yuppie to a
   bar but the wimp will still
   order a Perrier.

The grass is greener on the
   other side.

The dude across the street
   has better weed than you.

I'm on cloud nine.

I'm on angel dust.

A rolling stone gathers
   no moss.

It's hard to exchange bodily
   fluids with a jogger.

Don't make a mountain out
   of a molehill.

Don't make a castration out
   of a vasectomy.

People in glass houses
   shouldn't throw stones.

TV Evangelists shouldn't be
   so horny.

Politics makes strange
   bedfellows.

Beware of Senators bearing
   whips and chains.

Don't count your chickens
   before they're hatched.

Don't celebrate a Gold Medal
   before the urine test comes
   back negative.

Don't air your dirty linen in
   public.

Don't dump on your marriage
   on the Oprah Winfrey show.

A fool and his money are soon
   parted.

A fool and his money are soon
   taxed by Revenue Canada.

Don't bite your nose to spite
   your face.

Don't cut your head off to
   get rid of a zit.

There's no free lunch.

There's no free brunch.

Don't put the cart before the
   horse.

Don't put the car before
   the tow truck.

You can't see the forest for
   the trees.

You can't see the mall for
   the boutiques.

A bird in the hand is worth
two in the bush.

Larry Bird's jump shot is twice
as good as George Bush's.

An ounce of prevention is
worth a pound of cure.

An ounce of pretention is
a pound of manure.

Don't throw out the baby
with the bathwater.

Don't throw out the Trump
Tower with Donald Trump.

The straw that broke the
camel's back.

The parking ticket that got
you the Denver Boot.

You can't make an omelet
without breaking eggs.

You can't collect receivables for
the Mob without breaking legs.

You can't judge a book by its
cover.

You can't book a Judge for
sexual assault if he has a cover.

The early bird catches
the worm.

The early bird is the first
to defecate on your windshield.

You can't get blood from
a stone.

You can't get truth from the
National Enquirer.

No skin off my teeth.

No foreskin off my penis.

Always a bridesmaid, never
a bride.

Always a bridesmaid, never a
divorcée.

Discretion is the better part
of valour.

Don't make videos of
minors in hotel rooms.

Where there's smoke there's
fire.

Where there's smoke there's a
barbecue.

It is better to give than to
receive.

I'd rather be a hammer than a
nail.

Money is the root of all evil.

Poverty sucks.

The meek shall inherit
the Earth.

Our children shall inherit
the national debt.

Do unto others as you would
have them do unto you.

Do unto others before they do
unto you.

Tomorrow, and tomorrow   Shit happens.
Creeps in this petty pace from
day to day . . . It is a tale told
by an idiot, full of sound and
fury, signifying nothing.

If you "like" clichés, you'll "like" this puzzle. Finish off the follow-ing hackneyed expressions which have been hacked off at the word "like."

  1. eat like _____
  2. smoke like ____
  3. sleep like ____
  4. fit like ____
  5. melt like ____
  6. soar like ____
  7. blow up like _____
  8. cry like _____
  9. run like ____
10. shake like _____

27

NPL—A PUZZLE
IN A CONUNDRUM IN
AN ENIGMA

PICTURE IT. You walk into a crowded hotel room. There are people aged 18 to 80 ejaculating words (some four-lettered) and referring to each other as "Treesong," "Qaqaq," "Merlin," "Hart burn," "Twisto," "Sluggo," and "On and Off." You are not going mad, nor are you visiting the criminally insane. You are attending the *National Puzzler's League* (NPL) convention.

I had never heard of the NPL, but joined in 1991 at the suggestion of A. Ross Eckler (a.k.a. "Faro"), the editor of the language journal *Word Ways,* to which I am a regular contributor. The 1991 convention was being held at the Delta Chelsea Inn in Toronto, marking the first time a convention was being staged outside of the USA.

When I reached the check-in desk, I was asked my "nom" (pronounced by Americans to rhyme with Tom). A "nom" is a nom de plume which you are requested to select when you join the NPL. I picked the nom "Retrosorter" because of my interest in palindromes. (Check it out, it reads the same backwards as forwards, like Otto or Anna.) I felt somewhat silly introducing myself to the welcoming official by my nom and I grunted a barely audible "Retrosorter." This discomfort lessened when I noticed his name tag, "Ostrich," and it evaporated when he introduced me to

"Pebbles," and "Jo the Loiterer." Everybody is referred to by his or her nom. This democratizes matters when you're not sure how to address some Professor Emeritus.

The emphasis during the convention was on group word games and puzzles. For many this annual event is an opportunity to meet people who share a passion for constructing and solving word puzzles. It can be a humbling experience for the novice. We're not talking about people who solve the Sunday *New York Times* crossword. We're talking people who finish it within five minutes, and that's if they didn't compose the puzzle in the first place. The convention was hosted by one of the best constructors of cryptic crosswords, Torontonian Fraser Simpson ("Fraz"), with about 75 members out of a total membership of around 350 attending. Most members are Americans, but there are now 20 Canadian members, including nine from Ontario. There are also members from England, France, Italy and Israel. Many of the attendees are constructors and/or editors of puzzle publications. Others have shown superior skill in crossword competitions. Still others have appeared on quiz shows like *Jeopardy* or *Challenger*.

The convention programme had a Canadian flavour. One of the events was called *Maple Leaf Rag*. It featured puzzles composed by Canadians, some of them dating back to the 1920's. In one ecologically proper team event, we recycled some Toronto Stars in a search for specific categories like palindromes and paragraphs that contain all 26 letters in the alphabet.

The NPL was established on July 4, 1883 by a group of word puzzlers and was originally dubbed the Eastern Puzzlers' League. In 1920 "Eastern" was replaced by "National." It is the oldest puzzle organization in North America and one of the oldest in the world. It predates the creation of crossword puzzles by 30 years. Its official aim is "to provide a pastime of mental relaxation for lovers of word puzzles, and to raise the standard of puzzling to a higher intellectual level. . . ."

Each month the NPL puts out a puzzle magazine called *The Enigma,* which is sent to all its members. All the puzzles are made by NPL members, gratis. Teamwork is common in composing and solving puzzles. Deciphering the joint contributors and their addresses is a conundrum in itself. For example, when Jo the Loiterer of Basking Ridge, NJ, collaborated with Qaqaq of Atlanta GA, in a recent puzzle their joint "nom" and address became JAQ THE QATERER, Baskanta NA.

One of the most popular puzzle types is the rebus. In a rebus, a word or phrase is represented by letters, numbers or symbols. For example, 1 2 3 GO X could stand for "go fourth and multiply."

The NPL puts out a mini-sample of puzzles for prospective members. Try your luck at this rebus:

A 12-letter word is represented by the following equation.

$$T \overset{\bullet}{=} T$$

Most of the puzzles in *The Enigma* are designated as "flats." These puzzles should be written in well-metred verse but they can take a variety of forms. Here is a brief sampling of three types of flats (deletion, letter bank and charade), all of which appeared in *The Enigma* and all composed by Canadians.

Deletion: A word becomes a new one when an interior letter is removed. For example, if the word marked ONE = morose, the word marked TWO = moose.

Here is a sample puzzle composed by Fraser Simpson (Fraz): (Word marked BETs has 7 letters, the word marked BEST has 8 letters.)

> Our cause is just! We must be free!
> Attach this flyer to that tree.
> We'll cover BETs around the park
> (Though BEST may hurt their tender bark).

The context tells us that BETs has something to do with trees. Its answer is SAPLINGs; the answer to BEST is STAPLING.

Now try your luck at this deletion puzzle by Montrealer Rosalie Moscovitch (Wabbit).

The word marked DERRIERE has 6 letters; the one marked FRONT has 5 letters.

I shot a rock into the air:
It shattered Wilma's DERRIERE
Then struck her husband on the head
(Now she's a FRONT, 'cause Fred is dead.)

Letter Bank: From the "bank" of letters contained in the short word which has no repeat letters, a longer word is made using all the letters at least once and as many times as needed.

Example: Short word = SEA, Longer Word = ASSESSES.

The following letter bank was a joint effort of Wabbit and Mangie and appeared under the authorship of Wabbit. Word marked SHORT WORD has 6 letters; the one marked LONG WORD has 9 letters.

Will we all still be holding our SHORT WORD—oy vay—
As the same guy continues a LONG WORD away?
What is lost is BREATH. The long word is HEARTBEAT.

Now attempt this letter bank composed by Torontonian John R. Bird (Crowman):

The word marked ONE has 4 letters; the word marked TWO has
12 letters and is hyphenated into two equal parts of six.

When Tommy ONE his trousers on the TWO,
His Mommy made them just as good as new.

Charade: A longer word is broken into two or more shorter words. Example: ONE = HEAT, TWO = HEN   WHOLE = HEATHEN

I composed the following charades.
The WHOLE psychic needed support for his show.
So off to the neighbourhood church he did go.
His speech was persuasive: investment the word.
Parishioners decided to FIRST SECOND THIRD.
The answer is FUND/A/MENTALIST.

Try unravelling the following:

"A man's gotta do what a man's gotta do."
Rocky said, "Whoop da guy so's he's good black 'n blue."
This wasn't a WHOLE and it wasn't a threat.
Just the worst case of ONE TWO I've ever heard yet.

PART V

SO YOU THINK ENGLISH IS EASY, EH?

There's a popular misconception that the English language has become the dominant world language because it isn't complex. First of all, we must determine what we mean by English. Are we referring to American, Anglo-Indian, Australian, Black, British or Canadian English? And each of the myriad forms of English possesses varieties called dialects. True, English grammar is relatively simple, but this is where the simplicity ends. The idiomatic and jargonish nature of English is the bane of the non-native speaker. English possesses a wealth of homonyms with a myriad of meanings that are bound to addle someone trying to learn the language.

Speaking English is one thing; mastering it is another.

28

DON'T BITE THE DUST
OR SPILL THE BEANS OVER ENGLISH
IDIOMS

E NGLISH IS OFTEN characterized as being easy to learn as a second language because of its relatively simple grammar and syntax. It is also, by and large, unencumbered by inflection and gender markers. To listen to some Anglophiles, however, you'd think the English language were a gift from God. In fact, that's exactly what writer Steven Baker avers in the magazine *Writer's Digest*. Hungarian-born Baker declares, "No doubt English was invented in heaven. It must be the *lingua franca* of the angels. . . . English is probably the easiest language to learn. . . . Anyone who tells you it isn't so should take a trip around the world and listen to tongues wagging."

Richard Lederer echoes this position in *The Miracle of Language*. "People often say to me that English must be a very arduous and intimidating language for foreigners to master. How difficult can it be, I answer, when more than 350 million second-language users have learned to speak and understand it?"

Perhaps English is easy to speak, Mr. Lederer, but it certainly isn't easy to speak well. English possesses an insidious intricacy that defies logic. Some words can mean totally opposite things: to "sanction" can mean to forbid and to permit; to "dust" can mean to remove dust or to sprinkle with dust. "Literally" sometimes means literally, other times speakers use it to mean figuratively. "Sharp" speech means the same as "blunt" speech, and in the vernacular "hot" and "cool" connote the same thing. Responding to the language logically is not always recommended, as in retorting to "How do you do?" with the rejoinder, "How do I do what?"

English pronunciation is a struggle for the non-native speaker. The "th" sound is particularly difficult and a simple phrase such as "What's this?" is likely to be distorted. And it doesn't get any easier with the vowels. For example, the vowel sound found in "bird" or "nurse" occurs in virtually no other language.

Bill Bryson in *The Mother Tongue* characterizes English as a minefield for "the unwary foreigner. Any language where the unassuming *fly* signifies an annoying insect, a means of travel, and a critical part of a gentleman's apparel is clearly asking to be mangled." The highly idiomatic nature of English predisposes it to be mangled by the non-native speaker. The multiplicity of meanings to many of its common verbs like "get," "go," "make" and "put," especially when coupled with other words like "away," "off," "on" and "out," have frustrated many. Even when the phrase remains constant, the context can totally alter the meaning. Take the phrase "make up." The meanings of "make up to someone," "make up differences," "make up one's face" and "make up a story" are all different.

Idioms are illogical and many do not subscribe to the dictates of English grammar, let alone the rules of another language. Familiarity with a wide array of idioms and using them in their proper contexts is one of the major distinguishing marks of a native English speaker. Anthony Cowie points out in *The Oxford Dictionary of Current Idiomatic Usage* that it is "the tendency, especially in informal contexts, to prefer the Anglo-Saxon combination (e.g. "take up") to its singular Romance equivalent (e.g. "continue"), that makes mastering English very difficult for the non-native speaker."

Richard Lederer should be well aware of the difficulty English idioms pose for the non-native speaker. In *Anguished English* and *More Anguished English* he regales us with many English language signs found around the globe displaying idiomatic idiocy. A sign in an Acupulco hotel advertises that "the manager has personally passed all the water served here." A sign in a Tel Aviv hotel room reads "If you wish for breakfast, lift the telephone and our waitress will arrive. This will be enough to bring your food up." Some signs tell women what they can do, others what they cannot. Shoppers at a Hong Kong tailor shop are told that "ladies may have a fit upstairs." A sign in a Beirut hotel, on the other hand, reads that "ladies are kindly requested not to have their babies in the cocktail lounge." A Japanese hotel invites guests "to take advantage of the chambermaid," and a Tokyo hotel room gives the following heating (and not heated) instruction: "If you want just condition of warm, please control yourself." Prospective customers of a Bangkok dry cleaner are told to "drop your trousers here for best results."

Some curious English signs can be found in France. At one chateau, tourists are asked not "to invade Madame's private parts;" a Paris dress shop reads "dresses for street walking" and a French radio station signed off with, "we hope you have enjoyed our nocturnal emissions." If you need a drink in Thailand there's a place that advertises itself as "the shadiest cocktail bar in Bangkok," and a Tokyo bar advertises that it has "special cocktails for ladies with nuts." One might be loath to frequent the Zanzibar barbershop that advertises that "gentlemen's throats cut with nice sharp razors." Equally inviting is the Israeli butcher who says "I slaughter myself twice daily." If you buy a suit on the Greek island of Rhodes it isn't recommended to press the tailor for fast service. Why? "Because in big rush we will execute customers in strict rotation."

Lack of awareness of idioms can lead to less than desirable advertising and public relations, such as the Moscow hotel room sign that read "If this is your first visit to the USSR, you're welcome to it" and the following abrupt sign in the window of a Barcelona travel agent—"Go away."

Of all the world's languages, English possesses the largest vocabulary. The multitudinous variety afforded can, at times, be perplexing. Anthony Burgess in *A Mouthful of Air* points out that "French cannot say 'go up' or 'go down,' only *monter* or *descendre;* but at least those two words are firmly fixed in slots of unambiguous meaning. One feels that certain forms of English show a virtuosity that is more dazzling than helpful."

29

THE CLOUDS ARE
TWO LEVELS HIGHER THAN THEY
USED TO BE

I N A POST-GAME interview during the 1993 Stanley Cup play-offs, the star of the game, then-Canadiens member Paul DiPietro, was asked how he felt. He waggishly replied, "I'm on cloud seven"—seven being the highest level a 5'9" hockey player could attain. Actually, the highest rung in the expression, according to Linda & Roger Flavell, authors of *Dictionary of Idioms and their Origins* (Kyle Cathie, 1992), may indeed have been seven. In some parts of the USA "cloud seven" is still used and is a reference to the seventh heaven, the alleged residence of the Almighty.

Grammar codifies what is logical and predictable about language and allows us to make sense out of what otherwise would be random utterances. Idioms like "cloud nine," on the other hand, are not predictable and their meaning cannot be divined by looking at the individual words in the expression. The word idiom derives from the Greek *idios*, "one's own," "peculiar," "strange." Idioms are the bad boys, the rebels of language—they break all the rules. They are also, like gestures, what breathes life into language. One litmus test for an idiom is trying to translate it into another language: if, when translated, the expression doesn't retain its meaning, chances are it's an idiom, e.g. "kick the bucket."

How does an expression like "spill the beans" gain an idiomatic dimension? The Flavells tell us it is a process of transformation whereby an expression moves from its literal meaning to a metaphorical one before its idiomatic nesting. At one point, actual beans were spilled. The ancient Greeks were very choosy as to whom they accepted into their arcane clubs. A member would vote for admission of a candidate by depositing a white bean in a jar, and against by "black beaning" the candidate. Invariably, some clumsy member would knock over the jar, thus "spilling the beans" and revealing to all the level of opposition to the prospective member. The idiom "red herring" also shows the transformation from literal to idiomatic sense. After being dried, salted, and smoked, a herring acquires a reddish hue. Due to its odiferous nature, the herring was used in medieval times as a lure for training hounds to hunt deer. How did "red herring" acquire its modern sense of diverting attention away from a main argument? Credit for this goes to opponents of fox hunting, centuries later. To confuse the hounds chasing the foxes, anti-hunters would drag red herrings along the fox's trail to entice the olfactory-challenged hounds away from their quarry.

It is well-known that the idiom "thumbs-up" refers to the thumb position, and was a sign of approval that would delay passage of a defeated gladiator to the hereafter. Not so, say the Flavells. A turned-down thumb, or one closed in a fist, would grant life. Any other thumb position, including "up," meant the combatant was to be shown no mercy. According to Charles Funk, the reversal of meanings came as a result of a painting by French artist Jean Leon Gerome in 1873. He misinterpreted the death penalty sign, *Pollice Verso* (the title of the painting), as "thumbs down" rather than "thumbs turned."

The language of games has found widespread idiomatic usage, according to Robert Hendrickson in *Grand Slams, Hat Tricks & Alley-Oops* (Prentice Hall, 1994). The original "hat trick" was attained in cricket when a person bowled down three wickets with three consecutive balls and was then awarded a hat, or the proceeds collected in a hat. The term "alley-oop," used in basketball and football to refer to a high pass, was coined by American soldiers in France in World War I. It is a combination of the phonetic spelling of "allez" and "up" and means to lift something up.

The late Stuart Flexner said, "when you listen to America you hear baseball." Hendrickson believes you hear a lot more than the cracking of the bat. He states, "when you listen to English you hear rounders, cricket, rugby, football, horse racing, boxing, track and field, tennis and scores of other sports."

Some of the games our ancestors enjoyed were downright gruesome. The words "backbite" and "abet" derive from that popular medieval pastime, bearbaiting. The former referred to the attempt of dogs to bite a chained bear in the back of the head while he was busy trying to ward off a frontal attack. "Abet" was a "sic-em" signal to the dogs and derives from the Old French *abeter*, "to bait, to hound on." Bearbaiting was not the only genre of this "sport." Badgerbaiting involved putting a badger in a hole and then having dogs literally badger the poor badger to death. Hence, the verbal meaning of badger, "to harass."

Interestingly, many sports expressions undergo a metamorphosis. They are spawned as metaphors to describe an analagous situation outside the sport. When the expression picks up currency it acquires idiomatic status, and if it gets overused it obtains a hallowed state—that of being a cliché. That's the way the ball bounces.

Animals figure prominently in idioms, reflecting their greater importance historically in everyday life. Figure out which animal is being referenced by the clues.

* refers to the hidden animal

1. member of the family who has fallen out of favour is said to be the black * .
2. a secret source is a little * .
3. someone clumsy is described as a * in a ____   ____.
4. something that provides you with the wrong trail is said to be a red * .

5. when you reveal something unintentionally, you let the *
out of the _____.
6. very hot days are said to be * ____.
7. if you get someone in hot water, you _____ their * .
8. a person whose abilities are untested can be described as a
_____ * .
9. an unwanted cumbersome object is a white * .
10. an improperly examined purchase is a * in a _____.
11. in warding off hunger, you keep the * from the _____.
12. an ineffectual person is said to be a _____ * .

30

TO PLAY OR NOT TO PLAY,
THAT'S THE PITCH

To historian Jacques Barzun's famous maxim that "whoever wants to know the heart and mind of America had better know baseball," we can add "and its lingo." Imagine a spy eavesdropping on the following conversation:

Tom: I think Saddam is going to swing for the fences.

Bob: I think he's just throwing us a curve.

Tom: He has a history of playing hardball. It's right up his alley.

Bob: He must know if it goes into extra innings he'll get knocked out of the box and he's got no one in the bullpen.

Tom: Bob, the man's a screwball. He's got a history of pulling things from out of left field.

If our spy is not baseball literate, he's got at least two strikes against him. From its outset, baseball has infused American English with a myriad of expressions. Authors Joel Zoss & John Bowman in *Diamonds In The Rough* believe that baseball metaphors "have a resonance that Americans find both familiar and suggestive."

Israeli novelist A.B. Yehoshua states that national literatures exhibit particular motifs. He believes the crux of French literature is the relationship between a man and a woman; British literature's main focus is on class, and the major motif in American literature is the pursuit of the American Dream: Success. Many phrases that baseball has added to the language are metaphors for success. In a sense this is ironic, for in baseball, the best hitters fail in getting hits at least sixty-five percent of the time. If we're successful we're said to "have a lot on the ball," "a good batting average," a lot of "clout" or "moxie" and we "make a hit." "Batting a thousand" denotes the ultimate in success. To be successful we must have the "right stuff." We must perform "in the clutch," be a "gamer," "cover all the bases," and "put out." When the situation arises we must be prepared to "go to bat" for someone else. Since nice guys finish last, sometimes success entails "playing hardball." Conversely, if we are not successful, we "strike out," have an "off-day" or we're "out of our league" or "in a slump." If we lack "what it takes," we may be dubbed a "screwball" or a "bush-leaguer" or "minor-leaguer."

These same expressions are used by males to describe success or failure in the sexual arena. Success is shown by "getting to first base," and ultimate success is "scoring," or "going all the way." In dating, as in baseball, the ultimate humiliation is "striking out." Bradd Shore, in his article "Loading The Bases" (*The Sciences,* May/June 1990), points out that sexual metaphors apply only to the dating aspect of sex. A male would never boast about "going all the way" with a prostitute, nor talk about getting to "second base" with his wife. Shore states "the baseball metaphor doesn't apply to sex when sex is either fully domesticated and private, or when it is a fully public and commercial transaction. Baseball lingo is linked to sexual adventurism in dating behaviour, in which a male must negotiate a perilous field of play with at least the possibility of coming home to score."

Other sports make do with coaches, referees, and out-of-bounds; baseball needs managers, umpires and foul territory on top of that. In every other usage, "strike" means "hit;" only in baseball does it mean a miss. One associates most sports with harmonious sequences, like halves and quarters—not baseball. Baseball is oxymoronic and consistently asymmetrical. It is a totally "odd" sport. There are nine players and nine innings, a seventh inning stretch, a full count that totals five, and a total of three strikes. Also, baseball's sense of time is unique in North American sports by not being controlled by a set time period. A game can be played in ninety minutes; it could just as easily take four hours to complete. As Yogi said, "It ain't over till it's over." Unlike most sports, baseball's playing surface is also asymmetrical. The dimensions of an infield are dictated by rules, but not so the outfields, which vary considerably from ballpark to ballpark. In fact, the expression "ballpark figure" is used to describe an inexact estimation. To be "out in left field" describes a state of disorientation, suggesting the distance between the player and the action.

In his aforementioned article, Shore relates that even the use of verbs in baseball parlance is unique. There is a distinction between "playing" and "being." Strangely, merely "being" is more active than playing. The fielders "play," whereas the batter "is" at bat. The pitcher neither "is" nor "plays," he "pitches." One would never say that Nolan Ryan plays pitcher or that Willie Mays played at bat. Shore states that "the language of 'being,' rather than of 'playing' is also associated with proximity to 'home'." These conventions of speech reflect a world view in which "being" is linked to individual activity in a domestic, or home environment. In contrast, social role playing is linked to an "outer" field.

British writer Lesley Hazleton, attending her first baseball game at Yankee Stadium in 1979, recalled that as an English schoolgirl she had played a game somewhat akin to baseball called rounders. Rounders, however, lacked baseball's gusto. "The exhilaration of sliding into base! . . . The whole principle of hustle! . . . But for me the most splendid of these splendors was to watch the American language being acted out."

Many metaphors are drawn from sports. Identify the sport where the following expressions were originally used:

1. down to the wire
2. saved by the bell
3. one-on-one
4. at the drop of a hat
5. wild card

6. there's the rub
7. keep it up
8. shoot one's bolt
9. out of the blocks
10. blindsided

31

TO TWEAK OR TO PHREAK:
IT'S ALL GREEK TO NON-HACKERS

THOUGH SOME called him a *munchkin,* Waldo could hack with anybody, and as he opened the *condom* his thoughts turned to *frobnicating.* Soon he would advance to *tweaking* and *phreaking,* because his *studly* equipment was *bytesexual.* His only fear was that he would *bogotify* the program.

Welcome to the brave new world of cyberspeak. To help us understand this exotic dialect, Eric Raymond has provided us with *The New Hacker's Dictionary,* second edition (MIT Press, 1994). All the italicized words are entries in this dictionary. Raymond defines a "munchkin" as "a teenage-or-younger micro enthusiast hacking Basic or something else equally restricted." A "condom" is the plastic bag that protects the 3.5" diskettes. "Frobnicating" refers to unsophisticated manipulation of computer equipment, whereas "tweaking" implies fine tuning. "Phreaking" is the art and science of cracking phone networks, usually with the intent of making free long distance calls. "Studly" means powerful or impressive, and hardware is designated as "bytesexual" if it will pass its data on with a minimum of fuss. To "bogotify" is to make something bogus.

In the Jurassic Era of computers, if you needed a program only slightly different from an existing one, it was much faster to modify what you already had than to write a new one from scratch. This crude slicing up of a program to create a new one became the basis of the the verb "to hack." Standard dictionaries will usually imply a pejorative dimension to the word "hacker" as someone who gains access to a system illicitly. In computer circles, however, the term hacker is an esteemed designation and it denotes a true cyberphile who has a virtually zen relationship with his or her computer, transcending mere utilitarian application. To imply the illicit dimension of breaking into a system, hackers respectfully ask that the word "cracker" (as in safe-cracker) be substituted. Conversely, the term "user-friendly" is seen positively by mere mortals. Not so by hackers. Raymond defines it as "Programmer-hostile . . . systems that hold the user's hand so obsessively that they make it painful for the more experienced and knowledgeable to get any work done." Well, sorry!

Jargon in computer circles, as in most spheres, is used for inclusionary and exclusionary purposes. Knowing the lingo defines someone as a member of the illuminati; not knowing the arcana identifies you as an outsider and possibly a "suit." Raymond defines "suit" as "ugly and uncomfortable business clothing often worn by non-hackers. Invariably with a tie, a strangulation device that partially cuts off the blood supply to the brain."

Hacker lingo is more similar to the argot in the arts than the sciences because it also denotes sharing a level of consciousness. A "kluge" solution (from the German klug, clever) is characterized as a "clever programming trick intended to solve a particular nasty case in an expedient, if not clear, manner." This type of solution is dichotomized with an "elegant" solution, which "combines simplicity, power, and a certain ineffable grace of design." Raymond tells us that "the distinction is not only of engineering significance; it reaches back into the nature of the generative processes in program design. . . ."

Hackers seem to regard slang formation as a game and revel in its formation in a manner usually only displayed by children. For example, the word "gritch" means "complaint," and it is clearly a portmanteau of the words grouch and glitch.

Because so many computer terms are long, due to their technical nature, acronyms feature prominently in hackspeak. For example, the term Compact Disk Read Only Memory has been shortened into the more manageable CD-ROM. MIPS stands for "million instructions per second," a measure of computer speed. A WIMP environment stands for "Window, Icon, Menu, Pointing" device and my favourite, WOMBAT, stands for "Waste Of Money, Brains And Time" and refers to problems that are both boring and not worth worrying about. Normal grammatical conventions don't apply in the realm of cyberdom. As Raymond puts it, "All nouns can be verbed" (clipboard it over), . . . , and "all verbs can be nouned" (backflication). Hackers seem to regard adding the wrong suffix as a shibboleth and this leads to words like "mysteriosity" and "winnitude."

It is problematic when compiling a lexicon to decide what must be excluded because of space constraints. I am, nevertheless, surprised that Raymond chose to ignore a basic Internet term like "gopher" (the lookup device that lets you "tunnel" through the Internet) from this edition. Gophers originated as an information service at the University of Minnesota, home of the Golden Gophers varsity teams. Since its main role was to "go fer" things, gopher joined its rodent cousins mouse and hamster in having a computer connotation.

What do the following computer-related acronyms stand for?

1. BASIC	8. MB
2. CAD-CAM	9. MHZ
3. COBOL	10. OSCAR
4. CPS	11. PC
5. CPU	12. RAM
6. DOS	13. WYSIWYG
7. FF	

32

YOU'RE LIKELY TO
BE CLIPPED IN ENGLISH

I N *Hamlet,* Polonius informs King Claudius that "brevity is the soul of wit." If we can believe the results of a biblical study, it is also the soul of English. The number of syllables different languages require to translate the Gospel according to Mark were compared. Here are the results: English: 29,000; Teutonic languages (average): 32,650; French: 36,500; Slavic languages (average): 36,500; Romance languages (average): 40,200; Indo-Iranian languages (average): 43,100.

Richard Lederer, in *The Miracle of Language,* writes that "short words are bright, like sparks that glow in the night, prompt like the dawn that greets the day, sharp like the blade of a knife, hot like salt tears that scald the cheek, quick like moths that flit from flame to flame, and terse like the dart and sting of a bee."

If you're extremely perceptive, you'll have noticed that Lederer has chosen only monosyllabic words in this description. In fact, of the fifty most commonly used English words, not one of them is polysyllabic. Twenty words account for 25% of all spoken English words.

In 1066, the Normans invaded England. By the end of the fifteenth century, over 10,000 French words had come into the English language. Invariably, these words are longer than an equivalent Anglo-Saxon rooted word, e.g. "question" compared to "ask," "finish" compared to "end," and "difficult" compared to "hard." French also brought a wealth of technical words into English. Virtually all the words to describe government, law, and religion came from French. Old English was not particularly descriptive and French also provided a wealth of adjectives. There was a hierarchical structure between words of Anglo-Saxon derivation and those of French vintage. The humble trades like baker, miller, and shoemaker were of the former, while the more skilled trades like mason, tailor, and painter came from the latter. An animal while alive had an English name, e.g. sheep, ox, cow, pig. Becoming a meal francicized the animal into beef, mutton, veal, and bacon.

For all its borrowings, however, the soul of the language remained Anglo-Saxon. Linguist Albert Baugh wrote that regardless of class origins, everyone still "ate, drank and slept . . . worked, played, spoke, sang, walked, ran, rode, leaped and swam. They lived in houses with halls, rooms, windows, doors, floors, steps and gates . . . [A man's] spirit may [have been] French but his mind was still English as were nearly all his body parts: arms, legs, hands, feet, ears, eyes, nose, mouth, brain, liver, lungs, arse and ballocks."

As a result of the invasion by the Danes and the Normans two centuries later, 85,000 Anglo-Saxon words disappeared. This left only 4500 Old English words, which represent less than one percent of the words found in the *Oxford English Dictionary*. They are, however, the basic words of English, such as brother, sister, live, love, fight, man, wife and child. They also include many of the indispensable function words, such as at, but, for, in, on and to. The advantage of short words is that they take less time to say. Although intrinsically short, the English language employs a variety of techniques to shorten words even more. Chief among the shortening techniques is clipping. The verb "to dis" is increasingly transcending Black English usage as a shorthand way of saying "express disrespect for." In many cases the stumped version becomes more common than the original. Examples of this are "bra" instead of brassiere, and "flu" (which has the distinction of being clipped at both ends) instead of influenza. In some cases the original long word or phrase is totally abandoned, as in "pianoforte" which was shortened to "piano." Others in this genre include "zoological garden" (zoo), "cabriolet" (cab), "omnibus" (bus), "quacksalver" (quack), "pantaloons" (pants), "periwig" (wig), and "mobile vulgus" (mob).

Acronyms, in which the first letters or first syllables replace long phrases, is another shrinkage method. They are particularly prevalent in the field of technology. If laser radar was used recently in giving you a speeding ticket, you were done in by *Light Ampification by Stimulated Emission of Radiation, and RAdio Detection And Ranging.*

As a result of its borrowings from other languages, English is blessed with a large vocabulary that allows for a myriad of linguistic nuances. There are times, however, when we suffer from an overabundance of riches. Only thirty percent of English words in current use are of Anglo-Saxon origin. They are, however, the words that are most easily understood. Peter Farb, in *Word Play,* claims that in many classrooms half of the words used aren't understood, and that 80% of these non-understood words are of Latin and Norman derivation.

As iconoclast Mark Twain put it, "I never write metropolis when I can get the same for city. I never write policeman because I can get the same for cop."

What do the following acronyms stand for?

1.	ASAP	9.	REM
2.	CDROM	10.	SCUBA
3.	GIGO	11.	SNAFU
4.	MASH	12.	UNICEF
5.	NAFTA	13.	WASP
6.	NASA	14.	WAVES
7.	NATO	15.	ZIP
8.	NIMBY		

PART VI

DISTINCTLY CANADIAN

As in other domains, the English language in Canada is seen by outside observers as being somewhat indistinct, a hybrid of British and American influences. In fact, English Canadians travelling abroad are often taken for Americans. Gerald Clark has noted in *Canada: The Uneasy Neighbour* (1965), that although Canadians "seem indistinguishable from the Americans the surest way of telling the two apart is to make the observation to a Canadian."

Not only do Canadians follow trends, we create them. In 1993, I reviewed a book of neologisms that were on the cusp of being accepted for the first time in American language dictionaries. One of these "new words" was "multiculturalism," which has existed both as a word and a concept in Canada for thirty years.

33

QUEBEC ANGLOS INSIST
ON BEING REGARDED AS A
DISTINCT SOCIETY

The Oxford Companion to the English Language (OCEL) is missing an "s" at the end of its title. The *OCEL* has headings for over four hundred varieties of our multitudinous mother tongues, such as Australian English, Singapore English, Indian English and Black Vernacular English. I've never even heard of some of the varieties, such as Babu English, which is described in the *OCEL* as "a mode of address and reference in several Indo-Aryan languages, including Hindi, for officials working for rajahs, landlords, etc."

My mother tongue is actually one of these mutants listed in the *OCEL*. In my dealings with the outside world, I'm constantly being reminded of the distinctiveness of my English. After giving the American telephone receptionist my phone number, I said that my "local" was 222. She exclaimed, "Your what?" I quickly corrected myself and said, "my extension is 222." Similarly, I left a Newfoundland customer perplexed when I told him I would try to locate an item for him at one of our "filials" instead of using the word "subsidiaries."

I had just been guilty of speaking Quebec English.

It is taken for granted that English affects French. One hears terms like *le snack bar, chequer* instead of *vérifier,* and *un towing* (a tow truck). The French of the business world includes Anglicisms such as "meeting," "cash flow," "marketing," and "downsize." The prevalence of these Anglicisms is one of the reasons some Quebecois feel that their language is being threatened.

More and more, however, the flow isn't unidirectional. Many of the following are French terms in common use: *metro,* (the subway); CEGEP, *Collège des Études Générales et Practiques* (the system of junior colleges in Quebec); CLSC, *Centre Local des Services Communautaires* (local health and social services centre); *classes d'accueil* (welcoming classes); *caisse populaire* (cooperative bank); *péquiste* (member of the Parti Quebecois); *pure laine* (pure stock); and *depanneur* (convenience store). These are all terms that Quebec Anglophones are likely to use in their original form rather than translating them into English.

There are, however, many usages one hears which demonstrate that Quebec English is a real phenomenon. Yes, we Quebec Anglos are indeed a distinct society. As a demonstration of the difference of Quebec English, I've concocted the following.

"The *professor* (high school teacher) at the *polyvalent* (high school) believed that *scholarity* (schooling) was being affected by students consecrating (devoting) more time to *manifestations* (student demonstrations) about the dress code than to their *notes* (grades). During his *conferences* (lectures) their inattention was hurting their *apprenticeship* (learning).

He also felt he was getting *collaboration* (cooperation) from his *confreres* (colleagues) in better serving the *collectivity* (community). He thus had a *rendezvous* (meeting) with the *Director-General* (principal), Monsieur Langlois, and stated that it was a *primordial* (essential) consideration that some teachers be released before they reached *permanence* (tenure) under the *syndicate* (union) agreement. Monsieur Langlois stated that he was aware of the problem and had requested a *subvention* (grant) in the *annex* (appendix) to his *planification* (policy) budget to the *confessional* (denominational) school board in order that *formation modalities* (training methods) be created to make teachers more dynamic *animators* (group leaders).

Some of these terms, like collaboration, rendezvous and annex, could be used in non-Quebec English contexts, but I suspect words such as cooperation, meeting, and appendix respectively are more likely to be employed. This trend, I believe, coincides with the introduction of pro-French legislation in the province of Quebec. As a result, the usage of French has gained in prestige, making it more likely for Gallicisms to be adopted into English. Anglophones are speaking French to a greater extent at home and in the workplace, and this has created a situation where there may be greater familiarity with French usage of a certain term than the corresponding English usage. Thus, an Anglophone may use the word "demand" when he means "ask," "reparations" when he means "repairs," and "remark" when he means "notice," because he is constantly employing the words *demander, réparations,* and *remarquer,* when he speaks French.

Words that look the same in English and French often do not mean the same thing, e.g. *demander* means "to request," not "to demand." They are known as "faux amis," false friends, and often are confused by Anglophones speaking French and by Francophones speaking English. They are also many of the words liable to have their meanings changed in Quebec English. For example *résumer* doesn't mean "to resume," it means to summarize, and *décevoir* doesn't mean "to trick," it means to disappoint. Granted, not too many Anglophones in Quebec use resume and deceive in the French sense, but over time I suspect such usages will increase.

In many cases it's hard to know where English ends and French starts. Franglais includes such classics as "hot-dog steame all dressed" and a rock music review which declared that a group's appeal was to "male white trash de vieille souche." *Vieille souche* is a term that refers to "old stock" Quebecers. The concept of language purity is mythical. The reality is that English and French have been borrowing from each other since at least 1066 when the Normans invaded England. Ironically, some of the dreaded Anglicisms such as "rosbif" and "club" were Gallicisms that penetrated the English language in the eighteenth century.

34

NATIVE LANGUAGES
ARE LANGUISHING TOWARDS
OBLIVION

T HE ADJECTIVE "endangered" is usually twinned with the
noun "species." The onslaught of civilization has brought a
diminution in the planet's biodiversity. But not only are many
species on the verge of extinction, many languages are teetering
towards oblivion. Of the 6000 languages spoken, only 600 are considered likely to survive the end of the next century. A language is
considered secure if it has more than 100,000 speakers. One-third
of languages spoken today have fewer than 1000 speakers.

I spoke recently to Shirley Williams of the Native Studies
department of Trent University in Ontario, who said that only
three aboriginal languages in Canada are relatively secure: they
are Cree, Ojibway, and Inuktikut. Williams views this as a tragic
development. She believes that, since culture is intrinsically tied
to language, the loss of a language effectively destroys one's culture and leads to a diminishment of the very essence of life.

Many North American aboriginal words express spiritual con-
cepts that are not easily translated. For example, the word *mani-
tou* expresses a distinct concept of deity rooted in the force of
nature. Likewise, the Iroquoian word *ondinnonk* expresses a concept of a benevolent inner spirit that has no correlation in
English or French. Eli Taylor, an elder of the Sioux Valley reserve

in Manitoba, points out that "Native language embodies a value system about how we ought to live and relate to each other. . . . It gives a name to relations among kin, to roles and responsibilities among family members. . . . There are no English words for these relationships because your social and family life is different than ours."

A report published in 1990 for the Assembly of First Nations shows two-thirds of the 53 aboriginal languages spoken in Canada are at risk. More than half of the people surveyed can't communicate at all in their mother tongue and fluency declines greatly among the young. For example, the Mohawk bands of Kahnawake and Ahkwesasne have fluency rates of 96% in the 65 years and older category. In the 6-15 age group, however, the fluency rate drops to 23%.

There is a very clear sign when a language is in danger. Parents stop teaching it to children and children stop wanting to learn it. A child is unlikely to regard a language as important unless it is the dominant language of at least one of his or her parents. And according to a report put out by the Assembly of First Nations, the role of schools is limited. "No matter how much effort is put into school programs . . . the ultimate fate of the language is dependent on its use in everyday communication between the generations."

The loss of a language is not only a loss for a particular culture, it is a loss for the whole world. From other languages, we gain inspiration and ways of perceiving the world, and new words that don't exist in our own language. Kenneth Hale, an MIT linguist, puts it this way: "Languages embody the intellectual wealth of the people that speak them. Losing any of them is like dropping a bomb on the Louvre." According to Mark Pagel, a bio-mathematician at Oxford, different language communities have "particular habits of mind." He believes that learning a language may actually alter the brain, and he interprets the inability of Japanese adults to differentiate between the "la" and "ra" sounds as meaning that, on a physiological level, there are brain differences based on language. Thus, the extinction of a language could mean the loss to the world of a distinct brain structure.

In work pioneered by Noam Chomsky, linguists have been searching for a universal grammar, the rules common to all languages, genetically programmed in our brains. For example, it was once assumed that certain sentence structures were not possible. One could say "I will eat this kangaroo" but not "This will eat kangaroo I." Then someone "discovered" the Warlpiri of the Australian outback. Not only could tribesmen state, "This will eat kangaroo I" but "Kangaroo will this eat I" and "Eat will kangaroo this I." By observing which rules hold and which do not (e.g. "will" always comes in the second position in the sentence) linguists have been able to extend and better set the parameters of universal grammar. But to test and refine universal grammar, linguists need a myriad of examples from the grammars of diverse languages. Unfortunately, the database is shrinking dramatically.

Just as every species on the planet can't be preserved, neither can every language. All languages have a right to exist, but, as in nature, only some will survive. According to E. Sean Standing-Bear, whose American Osage tribe is reduced to a handful of elderly speakers, "Even if you create the ultimate curriculum, it cannot succeed unless you have economic development, extended families, and individuals that speak the language 90% of the time."

Many speakers of "minority" languages are going to opt to speak only the dominant "majority" language because they see this as the path to social and economic progress. Decades of language suppression have stigmatized many in their attitudes towards their mother tongues and they are unlikely to heed calls to help preserve a dying language. Saving any endangered language won't be easy. Perhaps what is needed is a policy of triage where the healthiest and the most critical languages are ignored and resources are devoted where they will prove most efficacious.

35

CP—THEN AND NOW

I N AN UNDERSTATED country like Canada, the Canadian Press is the quintessential Canadian organization. Unlike the logo of its American counterpart, the Associated Press (AP), the logo (CP) doesn't conjure up an image of a news organization. I asked fifteen semi-literate associates what the letters CP meant to them. The most popular answer was "Canadian Pacific," followed by "Communist Party." "Canadian Press" was answered by only one person. It even trailed "Colgate-Palmolive."

CP's definition for itself is as long as it is hyphenated: "the national news-gathering not-for-profit co-operative owned and operated by the daily newspaper industry." It was established in 1917 by Canadian publishers. On the occasion of its seventy-fifth birthday *The Canadian Press Stylebook* was extensively remodelled, and its mandate became: "To serve in English and French the newspapers that own it, and through them, the Canadian public." This is a distinct improvement over the redundant 1983 edition, which asserts that its task is "to deliver a domestic and international news report that is comprehensive, objective, impartial, accurate, balanced and fair."

It is hard to think of any news topic or journalistic situation that *The Stylebook* hasn't covered in its 471 pages. It is replete with a myriad of information. It tells you the difference between a lutz and an axel, explains the Richter scale, gives guidelines for the press' dealing with the police, and explains why Aspirin has a capital A in Canada (Sterling Drugs owns the Aspirin Canadian trademark). It tackles all the knotty grammatical matters so that Canadian journalists "can get on with writing their best prose."

One of my favourite lines in the Stylebook is the following in the Libel section: "Except in Quebec, it is virtually impossible to libel the dead." No wonder René Levesque told all Quebecers to take a valium. In Quebec, even the dead are touchy.

Another curious line concerning the dead occurs in the Obituaries section. Under the Funerals subsection we are told "not to suggest that the remains are in any way the person."

Although Canadian Press was formed in 1917, it was not until 1940 that a short guidebook was written with the quaint title *A Guide for Writers and Filing Editors*. A "filing editor" was "responsible for all the news going to member papers on his wire, and seeks to assure that a complete report conforming with standards of the service is filed." He is "continually reshuffling his copy in the order of its importance." This constant juggling is the "talent by which a filing editor justifies his key position," and, I suppose, his inflated 1940 weekly salary of $45.00.

The 1992 introduction states that the *Stylebook* was redone to "reflect the priorities and sensitivities of the 90's. . . ." In the chapter entitled "Sensitive Subjects" some of the delicate subjects include age, disabilities, race and sexism. Such sensitivities are not reflected in the 1940 guidebook, where they appeared only in a "Use of Words" section. "A member of the black race is called a 'Negro,' not 'colored'." In the "Preferred—or Correct" subsection we are instructed to favour "Chinese" over "Chinaman," and "Japanese" over "Jap." The terms "Reds," and "Canada's young defenders" are considered to be "editorial expressions unless attributed to those who use them."

The 1992 edition states that news stories should be "free of explicit or unconscious racism" and should "identify a person by race only when it is truly pertinent." The terms "Jew" and "Negro" should be used for both sexes, not "Jewess" or "Negress" for women. What to call Native people is problematic. The term "Indian" is regarded as offensive by some Natives. To complicate matters, some Natives don't like the term "native." Whenever possible the "actual name of a native community—Cree, Mohawk, etc., should be used."

Sexism is also not an issue in the 1940 guidebook. This is not surprising considering that the word sexism is first found in dictionaries in the mid-sixties. The only reference to women I could find is the use of "widow" being preferred over "wife" when describing the "former mate of a dead man." The subject of sexism is handled in detail in the new edition. The cardinal rule is to "treat the sexes equally and without stereotyping." As an example, it declares that the adjectives attractive, leggy, or bosomy are as inappropriate in describing a woman as the expressions hunk, hairy-chested, and having great buns are in describing a man. We are instructed to use businesswoman, Frenchwoman, and newspaperwoman, but to eschew journeywoman and second basewoman. On the prickly subject of how to refer to non-heterosexuals, we are told to go with the "individual's preference when it is known. Prefer sexual orientation to sexual preference; gay people do not view their sexuality as an option . . . and to consider same-sex as an alternative to homosexual or gay."

In the 1940 "Use of Words" section we are told to "place a wreath" but never to "lay it." The following words are found in the "Under the Ban" heading with the following caveat: "Though not all demonstratedly improper or incorrect, the following words are not wanted in the CP report." The "banned" words include contacted, educator, motivated, quite, reportedly, socialite and (the very pernicious) very. Included as trite expressions to which "any alternative is an improvement" are dramatic, for the purpose of, and went to the polls. In the spelling section we are told to prefer Nazism over Naziism, skis over skiis and, surprisingly, to choose cigaret over cigarette.

Lest anyone think there is not a Canadian imprint on the 1940 book, the following protectionist sentiment should assuage their concerns. "Vulgarisms from south of the border are banned. 'Like' is not a conjunction, and 'We do not have' is not optional for 'We have not'."

So the next time you are asked at the border whether you did any cross-border shopping, as a proud Canadian, just lift your head and declare, "We have not!"

36

WHAT A DIFFERENCE AN
S-WORD MAKES

T HE LATEST four-letter Canadian political word is missing a
letter. The taboo word is CUT. No politician wants to admit
that a social program is going to be "cut." It's too uncouth. In its
place we've gotten a variety of long substitutions, like "redesign,"
and "modernize." Health Minister Diane Marleau has made a
contribution to the obfuscation of the word "cut." Recently, she
expressed her concern over the provincial governments' "*delisting*
of services."

George Orwell said that political language "is designed to
make lies sound truthful and murder respectable, and to give an
appearance of solidity to pure wind." And the north Canadian
wind blows as forcefully as any international gust. Typical is the
language used in the following memorandum issued to Ontario
auditors for Revenue Canada in the 1980s that said quotas aren't
quotas when they're "materiality of adjustments in relation to
assigned workloads."

Given the usual hackneyed nature of political discourse, there
was a brief period in 1994 when the level of political debate
in Quebec was downright substantial and respectable. Lucien
Bouchard, on a visit to Washington and the United Nations in
March 1994, talked of "secession" and "independence." Bouchard

stated, "I felt it was essential to talk straight and not play around with words, saying we aren't separatists, we're sovereignists." Around the same time, in an interview with *The Economist,* Jacques Parizeau described himself as a "separatist," eschewing the softer word "sovereignist." Alas, this atypically honest political language was not to last. An Angus Reid poll held in late March '94 showed clearly that running on a separatist platform could cost the Parti Quebecois the election. Hence, the weasel word "sovereignty" ruled sovereign once again.

Sovereignty has been one of the fuzziest words in the political lexicon for the past two decades. A CROP poll in 1992 found that 20% of Quebecers believed that they would still be electing MPs to Ottawa after Quebec became a sovereign state. Sociologist Maurice Pinard interviewed Montrealers on the meaning of the word sovereignty just prior to the sovereignty-association referendum of 1980. Confusion on the word's meaning was so high that some people believed there was a link between sovereignty and the Sovereign—Queen Elizabeth!

The problem and the political attraction of a word like sovereignty is that its meaning is imprecise and doesn't commit one to a course of action where one chooses A over B. Norman Webster wrote in a March 12, 1994 *Gazette* article that sovereignty "implies that one can get what one wants, run one's own affairs, yet not do anything radical or rupturing to the existing order."

It is not only Canadian society that has found the word appealing. William Safire, on January 6, 1991, in his *New York Times* "On Language" column, related that before the break-up of the Soviet Union there was a move afoot to have the word "Sovereign" as part of the title of the State. One group from Kazakhstan wanted to jettison the word "Socialist" and create the "Union of Soviet Sovereign Republics." Another delegation wanted to excise the word "Soviet," meaning "council," because of the word's association with the Bolshevik Revolution. Their suggestion for the name of the new country was "Union of Sovereign Socialist States." Needless to say, the total break-up of the U.S.S.R. preempted the need for either of these two "Sovereign" proposals.

The term sovereignty had an interesting political connotation in the United States just prior to the Civil War. "Pop-Sov" (popular sovereignty) was a slogan used by Abraham Lincoln's Democratic opponent Stephen Douglas in the 1860 presidential race to refer to local decision-making without separation. It referred to Douglas' position that slavery could be extended into new areas if those territories voted to do so.

The word "soverein" came into the English language in 1290 from the Old French *soverain,* which in turn derives from the Latin *super,* "above, over." The word soon acquired a "g" and became "sovereign," because people assumed that a sovereign must reign. As a noun it referred to the recognized supreme ruler of a people. As an adjective it meant "supreme," standing out above others as in a "sovereign leader." It seems to have acquired a venerated position in many languages because not only does it describe who is supreme politically but who *should* be supreme. Over the centuries sovereignty became centred in "the people," instead of being personified in a "sovereign ruler." Louis XIV could declare such a state of affairs in *"L'État c'est moi,"* but after the French Revolution the people declared "We are France." Being against sovereignty had become akin to being against democracy or motherhood.

Ironically, as the nations of the world bind themselves in international agreements, the concept of sovereignty allowing a state to act independently is becoming anachronistic. William Safire, in his aforementioned column, quoted former American Secretary of State George Shultz who said that nations "have accepted limitations on their sovereign rights to act as they choose . . . affected powerfully by technology, by the way borders are becoming porous, almost irrelevant, in more and more areas of sovereign importance: money, ideas, information, missiles."

And you thought Sovereignty-Association was an oxymoron.

ANSWERS

Chapter 3
1. cucumber 2. beet 3. apple 4. cauliflower 5. rhubarb
6. grapes 7. beans 8. peach 9. peas 10. banana

Chapter 5

1=p	2=c	3=l	4=g	5=k	6=h	7=f	8=m	9=i
10=j	11=a	12=b	13=o	14=e	15=d	16=n		

Chapter 6

1=b	2=c	3=h	4=e	5=j	6=l	7=g	8=n	9=a
10=k	11=i	12=d	13=m	14=f				

Chapter 9

1=i	2=j	3=b	4=c	5=h	6=a	7=k	8=g	9=f
10=l	11=e	12=d						

Chapter 11

1=d	2=f	3=h	4=a	5=g	6=j	7=l	8=c	9=e
10=k	11=b	12=i						

Chapter 12
1. If you sleep with dogs, you'll wake up with fleas.
2. Live and let live.
3. United we stand, divided we fall.
4. An ounce of prevention equals a pound of cure.
5. Candy is dandy but liquor is quicker.
6. Don't look a gift horse in the mouth.
7. Beauty is skin-deep.
8. Beware of Greeks bearing gifts.
9. Practice what you preach.
10. Beggars can't be choosers.

11. You can run but you can't hide.
12. Physician, heal thyself.

Chapter 13
1=b   2=f   3=i   4=e   5=h   6=l   7=a   8=k   9=j
10=g   11=c   12=d

Chapter 15
1. excessive, incorrect 2. warning 3. possible 4. inconsistent
5. lively 6. realistic 7. disappoint 8. claim 9. sentence
10. sensitive

Chapter 16
1. Sam 2. toil, tears and sweat 3. will gather 4. fibs 5. asketh
6. the multitude of counsellors 7. The woman that deliberates

Chapter 17
1. living *dead* 2. guest *host* 3. Pale *Fire* 4. long *shorts*
5. peace *offensive* 6. rolling *stop* 7. good *grief*
8. light *heavyweight* 9. Sounds of *Silence* 10. True *Lies*

Chapter 18
1. Sinai, Canaan 2. hieroglyphics 3. Philistines 4. Mongols
5. Acropolis 6. hemlock 7. lava, Vesuvius 8. braziers 9. bubonic
10. armada 11. circumnavigated 12. Don Quixote 13. spinet

Chapter 19
  1. It's fun to be bound/bound to be fun
  2. Shaming of the true/taming of the shrew
  3. Arm bears/bear arms
  4. Work is the curse of the drinking class/drink is the curse of
     the working class
  5. goalie host/holy ghost
  6. Beijing rule/Raging Bull
  7. frontal lobotomy
  8. the wrath of grapes/The Grapes of Wrath
  9. To mock a killing bird/To Kill a Mockingbird
 10. Can't feel the beating/Can't beat the feelin.'

Chapter 23
1. ant aunt 2. tick tic 3. mite might 4. earn ern
5. mussel muscle 6. whale wail 7. towed toad 8. sole soul
9. dear deer 10. doe dough 11. moose mousse 12. gnus' news
13. hare hair 14. lyin' lion 15. lynx links 16. cheetah cheater
17. mare mere 18. hoarse horse 19. boar bore
20. gorilla guerilla

Chapter 24
1. tribulations 2. purposes 3. desist 4. choose 5. done with
6. every 7. void 8. sound 9. foremost 10. means 11. vigour
12. byways 13. behold 14. ruin 15. caboodle 16. proper 17. cry
18. wooly

Chapter 25
1. level 2. Civic 3. Laval 4. Menem 5. Seles 6. noon 7. redder
8. kayak 9. deified 10. a Toyota 11. put up 12. race car
13. pull up 14. able was I ere I saw Elba

Chapter 26
1. a bird, a pig 2. a chimney 3. a log, a baby 4. a glove 5. butter
6. an eagle 7. a balloon 8. a baby 9. a deer 10. a leaf

Chapter 27
Rebus: periodontist (period [.] on "T" = "T")
Deletion: "derriere" = window, "front" = widow
Letter Bank: tore, teeter-totter
Charade: malediction, male diction

Chapter 29
1. sheep 2. bird 3. bull (in a) china shop 4. herring
5. cat (out of the) bag 6. dog days 7. cook (their) goose
8. dark horse 9. elephant 10. pig (in a) poke
11. wolf (from the) door 12. lame duck

Chapter 30
1. horse racing 2. boxing 3. basketball 4. boxing 5. football
6. bowling 7. badminton 8. archery 9. foot racing 10. football

Chapter 31
 1. <u>B</u>eginner's <u>A</u>ll-Purpose <u>S</u>ymbolic <u>I</u>nstruction <u>C</u>ode
 2. <u>C</u>omputer-<u>A</u>ided <u>D</u>rafting; <u>C</u>omputer-<u>A</u>ided <u>M</u>anufacturing
 3. <u>C</u>ommon <u>B</u>usiness-<u>O</u>riented <u>L</u>anguage
 4. <u>C</u>haracters <u>P</u>er <u>S</u>econd
 5. <u>C</u>entral <u>P</u>rocessing <u>U</u>nit
 6. <u>D</u>isc-<u>O</u>perating <u>S</u>ystem
 7. <u>F</u>ast <u>F</u>orward
 8. <u>M</u>ega<u>b</u>yte
 9. <u>M</u>ega<u>h</u>ertz
10. <u>O</u>ptical <u>S</u>canning <u>R</u>eader
11. <u>P</u>ersonal <u>C</u>omputer
12. <u>R</u>andom <u>A</u>ccess <u>M</u>emory
13. <u>W</u>hat <u>Y</u>ou <u>S</u>ee <u>I</u>s <u>W</u>hat <u>Y</u>ou <u>G</u>et

Chapter 32
 1. <u>a</u>s <u>s</u>oon <u>a</u>s <u>p</u>ossible
 2. <u>c</u>ompact <u>d</u>isc <u>r</u>ead <u>o</u>nly <u>m</u>emory
 3. garbage <u>in</u>, garbage <u>o</u>ut
 4. <u>m</u>obile <u>a</u>rmy <u>s</u>urgical <u>h</u>ospital
 5. <u>N</u>orth <u>A</u>merican <u>F</u>ree <u>T</u>rade <u>A</u>greement
 6. <u>N</u>ational <u>A</u>eronautics and <u>S</u>pace <u>A</u>dministration
 7. <u>N</u>orth <u>A</u>tlantic <u>T</u>reaty <u>O</u>rganization
 8. <u>n</u>ot <u>i</u>n <u>m</u>y <u>b</u>ackyard
 9. <u>r</u>apid <u>e</u>ye <u>m</u>ovement or <u>r</u>oentgen <u>e</u>quivalent in <u>m</u>an
10. <u>s</u>elf-<u>c</u>ontained <u>u</u>nderwater <u>b</u>reathing <u>a</u>pparatus
11. <u>s</u>ituation <u>n</u>ormal, <u>a</u>ll <u>f</u>ouled <u>up</u>
12. <u>U</u>nited <u>N</u>ations <u>I</u>nternational <u>C</u>hildren's <u>E</u>mergency <u>F</u>und
13. <u>w</u>hite <u>A</u>nglo-<u>S</u>axon <u>P</u>rotestant
14. <u>W</u>omen <u>A</u>ccepted for <u>V</u>olunteer <u>E</u>mergency <u>S</u>ervice
15. <u>z</u>one <u>i</u>mprovement <u>p</u>lan

AUTHOR'S BIOGRAPHY

Howard Richler is a regular contributor to the "Speaking of Language" column in *The Gazette* and to the *Dell Champion* puzzle publication. He recently published *The Dead Sea Scroll Palindromes,* illustrated by Danny Shanahan of *The New Yorker.* He keeps himself otherwise busy in his day job as director of sales for the multinational steel company, Acier Leroux Inc.